the weekend cook

matthew evans
photography by alan benson

the weekend cook

RANDOM HOUSE AUSTRALIA

contents

the
slow
weekend

THE FINEST TEA SHOP

6 Flavour Tea Blends

HOME MADE JAM AND HOT SCONES

WITH FRESH CREAM

~~get up late~~
buy socks
clean gutters
~~carrots~~
growers mkt sat
have kids
write novel

the weekend cook

Weekends. Our time. Time off. Fewer deadlines, fewer cares, more hours in the day for the family, the lover, those friends you've been meaning to have over. More time for real food cooked with tenderness and served with passion.

Weekends are the best time to cook. You can imbue food with more of your soul. Slowly braise meats, cook pulses from scratch, perhaps try a recipe that differs from your usual repertoire. Most of all, you can dance the way you want to in front of the stove, sing into the rolling pin, play air guitar, avoid processed foods and poke your tongue out at the world… all while the soup simmers or the biscuits bake.

Because food has such an emotional connection, I've divided the weekend into five types. First up comes the lost weekend, where you're feeling just a little less like facing the world than you do a rhubarb crumble flecked with pistachios. Next comes the inevitable busy weekend, when all those things you pack into your time off (and your kids' time off) mean you don't necessarily have hours to spend in front of the stove, but by jeez you want to eat well when you finally come to rest. There's the romantic weekend, when you rekindle old flames or ignite new ones, complete with a pancake recipe that promises to help fan that burning desire. I've given recipes to suit the social weekend, when you finally get someone over for brunch or lunch or dinner. And to finish I've celebrated the slow weekend, where you've the time to potter about while the beans soften and the meats cook to buttery tenderness. Of course each of your weekends may be a mixture of types. And that's just the way it should be, because it's your time, and you make the rules. Or break them.

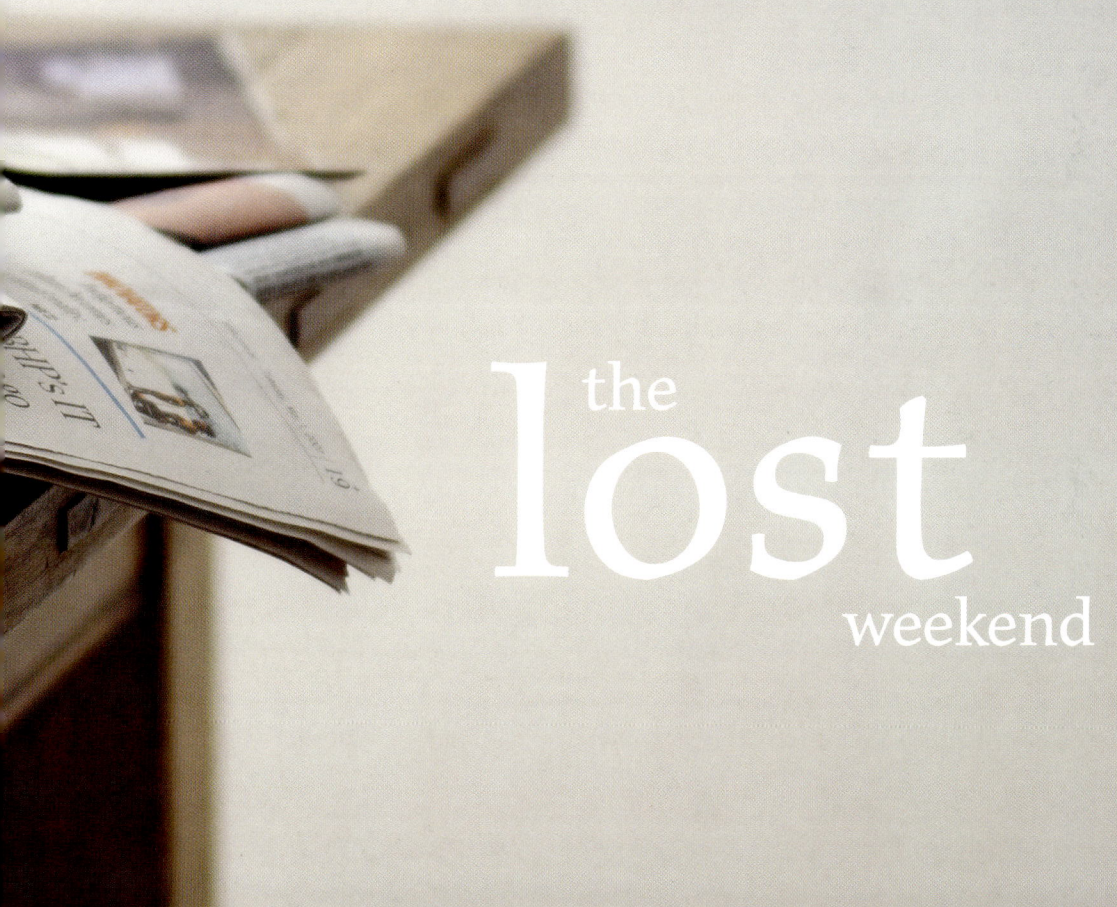

the
lost
weekend

Close the door. It's a day of rest. A day when the rest can do whatever they like but I'm pretending to be a hermit. It's a hangover day. Or an I-don't-want-to-deal-with-it day. The Lost Weekend is a time of selfish indulgence, of doona days when the world can revolve around your home, your mood. A time of nesting, of reading every single page of the paper. Of hot water bottles, warm milk and granny rugs over your legs. It's a mellow weekend, where the home is the cocoon, where there's solace to be found in a humble soup and a whole lot of love to be found in chocolate mousse.

Isn't it funny. Weekdays we shower, shave and dress smart.
Weekends, it's crumpled T-shirts and unkempt hair. I guess
we spend our downtime dressed like slobs because we know
our loved ones love us the way we really are.

rich mushroom omelette with gruyère
(serves 2)

butter, for frying
2 medium-sized flat mushrooms, diced
salt and freshly milled black pepper

5 eggs
40g (2-3 tablespoons) grated gruyère
  or equivalent

cooking time: 5 minutes

Heat a knob of butter in a large omelette pan and fry the mushrooms really well, adding
a little salt and pepper as they cook. They will go dark, and soft, then eventually dry out a
little, all while the flavours intensify.

Remove and put into a mixing bowl. Whisk the eggs into the mushroom mixture, adding
more salt and pepper to taste.

Heat some more butter in the omelette pan and when it starts to brown, add the egg
mixture all in one lot, constantly stirring the base of the pan so the mixture is always getting
to a new, hot part. This makes the omelette cook through better. When it's starting to get
firm throughout, but is still a little runny, stop stirring and scatter over the grated gruyère.
Keep over a medium flame to brown the bottom, then fold over by tilting the pan and
running a spatula around from the top. It may take a bit of encouraging.

Invert onto a plate and cut in half. Serve with a glass of sauvignon blanc, if you're up to it,
along with some fresh bread for dipping in the (hopefully) still moist centre.

Acquacotta is one of the most unassuming soups. It doesn't need stock and can be as simple or as complex as you like. This version relies on good bread, ripe tomatoes, and great olive oil. If you don't have these, and some decent cheese, cook something else.

acquacotta
(serves 4)

65ml ($1/_4$ cup) extra virgin olive oil
2 medium onions, peeled and chopped
2 large (about 400g) extremely ripe tomatoes, chopped (tinned are better than unripe fresh tomatoes)
about $1^1/_2$ teaspoons salt and some freshly milled black pepper

40g finely grated Italian parmesan (a good cheddar could also work, but not as effortlessly)
4 eggs
4 thick slices peasant-style bread
roughly 8 basil leaves, torn

cooking time: 20 minutes

Heat half of the olive oil in a large saucepan and fry the onions until nice and soft. Slop in the tomato, salt, pepper and 1 litre of water and simmer for a good 15 minutes.

Whisk the parmesan and eggs together and season a little with pepper and possibly more salt.

Chargrill or toast the bread until it's dark but not burnt and place in the bottom of four large bowls (rub the bread with a raw garlic clove at this point, if you like).

Add the basil to the boiling soup along with the remaining olive oil. Pour the egg mixture over the bread, then ladle the soup over the top. It will cook the egg, melt the cheese a little and soak into the bread. Serve immediately.

Life is not like the movies. My childhood dream of becoming a chook farmer is going to plan like a Hollywood marriage. I'm as level-headed as a lead in a Woody Allen flick. Thankfully, there's always solace in the kitchen. And toast soldiers for dipping.

coddled eggs with herbed cheese and chives

(serves 1)

1 egg (preferably free-range)
$1/_2$ oven-roasted or semi-dried tomato,
   cut into little pieces
1 tablespoon fetta or goat's cheese

1 teaspoon fresh herbs, chopped
   (use basil, oregano, parsley)
1 teaspoon chives, snipped

cooking time: under 10 minutes
you'll also need: little 200ml heatproof dishes to cook them in, or use little cups

Butter the inside of a tiny individual ceramic serving dish (just big enough for an egg and its topping) and crack an egg into it. Top with the tomato, crumbled cheese, herbs and chives.

Place ceramic dish in a saucepan, with simmering water halfway up the sides of the dish, and cook with a lid on, for 6-8 minutes or until cooked the way you like it. Runny is yummy.

An infectious laugh. A stern, feminine glance. Trust.
A long lunch. A bloody marvellous hangover cure.
Some things are made to share.

ham, provolone and mustard fried sandwich

(serves 2)

2 teaspoons Dijon mustard
1 tablespoon butter, softened
4 thick slices quality white bread
enough sliced provolone or cheddar to
    cover the bread well

2 decent slices of leg ham
pickles or gherkins, sliced
good sprinkling smoked paprika
extra butter, for spreading and frying
2 eggs

cooking time: 5 minutes

Mix the mustard and butter together well. Top two slices of bread with cheese, ham, and pickle. Spread the mustard mixture on the other slices, sprinkle well with smoked paprika. Put both pieces of bread together, fillings facing in, to make a sandwich. Butter the top slice of bread, then slide the sandwich, butter-side down, into a non-stick frypan and cook gently until brown. Butter the side facing up before turning it over to brown, too.

In the same pan, fry the eggs to your liking, pop on top of the sandwiches, then serve with a little roasted or grilled tomato.

Imagine a world without truffle oil. It's easy if you try.
No plastic cheese slices, and real meat in pies. Imagine a
world without bullies as leaders, a place full of cuddles and
rich with song. Imagine a dinner there, and invite me along.

spaghetti with pork, fennel and tomato
(serves 4)

1 tablespoon olive oil
2 cloves garlic, crushed
400g tin crushed tomatoes
about 200g pork and fennel sausage mince
   (otherwise use 200g coarsely ground pork
   sausage mince mixed with 2 teaspoons
   lightly crushed fennel seeds)

500g spaghetti
a good grating of mild pecorino or
   Italian parmesan
freshly milled black pepper

cooking time: 15 minutes

Heat the olive oil in a small pan and fry the garlic gently for a minute. Add the crushed tomatoes and simmer 10 minutes.

When ready to eat, cook the pasta in 5 litres rapidly boiling water, which has loads of salt in, until it's al dente – still firm to the bite.

While the pasta cooks, crumble the sausage meat (and fennel seeds) into the simmering sauce and cook through. Stir in the drained cooked pasta, with a little of its cooking water to prevent it becoming dry. Serve with grated pecorino and pepper.

Maybe it's a boy thing. Or a lost weekend thing. But a big night out deserves a big sandwich the day after.

steak sandwich with barbecued pumpkin

(serves 1)

1 minute steak (try rump)
a pinch paprika (preferably Spanish)
4-5 thin slices peeled pumpkin
vegetable oil for cooking

$1/_4$ onion, peeled and finely sliced
2 thick slices dense, chewy bread
BBQ sauce
chickpea aïoli (see page 24)

cooking time: 10 minutes

Preheat the barbie (or heat a big pan).

Dust the steak with the paprika. Rub it, and the pumpkin, with some salt and pepper and brush with oil. Chargrill the pumpkin and brown the onion on the hotplate. When they're ready, start to cook the steak. Minute steak usually means it takes less than a minute.

Stack up all these cooked goodies on one slice of bread. Add BBQ sauce to taste.

Smother the other side of the bread generously with the chickpea aïoli, press on top and eat the lot, trying not to drip too much juice, or "ooh" and "aah" too loudly.

Give me garlic. Give me an egg. Give me a tin of pulses and in just a few minutes I'll give you a wonderful paste for smearing, dipping, or drizzling.

chickpea aïoli

(makes enough for 4 to 5 steak sandwiches)

100g cooked chickpeas (tinned are okay), well-rinsed
1 egg yolk
2 teaspoons lemon juice or wine vinegar

1 teaspoon Dijon mustard
4 cloves roasted garlic (or use 2 fresh)
125ml ($^1/_2$ cup) extra virgin olive oil
salt and freshly milled black pepper

preparation time: 5 minutes

Place chickpeas, yolk, lemon juice, mustard and garlic in a food processor and blend.

With the motor running, add the olive oil in a steady stream. Add salt and pepper to make it zappy enough for your tastes, and lick a bit off your fingers to really appreciate it.

While this aïoli is really good on a steak sandwich (see page 23), it's also great for serving with fried cauliflower, grilled lamb or as a dip.

What I need is a pair of daks I can wipe my hands on as I cook. I'd love a white linen shirt that doesn't show spag bol stains. Give me clothes that repel posset – that little bit of themselves that babies love to leave behind. We can think about fashion later.

polpette italian-style pork, veal and sage meatballs
(serves 3 to 4)

500g mixed pork and veal mince (not too lean or the patties will turn out dry) or beef mince (it will give a lesser result)
2 eggs
about 2 tablespoons chopped fresh sage leaves
$1/_2$ teaspoon salt and a big fat pinch freshly milled black pepper

50g (roughly 5 fine slices) prosciutto, finely diced
25g (2-3 tablespoons) finely grated Italian parmesan
olive oil, for frying

cooking time: 10 minutes

In a large bowl mix the mince with the eggs, sage, salt, pepper, prosciutto and parmesan. Use your well-washed hands to make sure the mixture is thoroughly mixed (if you don't, you could end up with one salty bit, one sagey bit, one cheesy bit).

Gently heat a little oil in a large, heavy-based frypan. Form the mince mixture into golf ball sizes then press if you want them to cook quicker to form nice patties. Fry, in batches, until well browned and cooked through.

Serve with tomato-based sauce or as part of an antipasto. As big patties they're good tucker for a barbie, as small balls they're perfect for tossing through spaghetti.

26

There was a time before you were the kids' taxi. A time when grommets were more interested in licking cheesecake mix from the spatula than mucking about with a Wii. A time when one day's roast lamb became the next day's shepherd's pie.

real shepherd's pie
(serves 6)

40g butter
2 medium onions, peeled and finely diced
2 medium carrots, peeled and finely diced
2 sticks celery, finely diced
3 tablespoons or more tomato paste
500g leftover cooked lamb, finely diced
  or minced

80ml ($^1/_3$ cup) Worcestershire sauce
1 tablespoon white wine vinegar
1 sprig thyme
1 bay leaf
all the left over gravy from the roast
1kg potato, mashed the way you like it
melted butter, for brushing

cooking time: allow 30 minutes before assembling and 30 minutes after
you'll also need: a 2-3 litre, 5cm tall casserole dish or similar

Preheat the oven to 200°C.

Heat the butter in a big pot and fry the vegetables until soft, about 10 minutes, without allowing them to darken too much. A lid helps speed this up.

Stir in the tomato and fry to brown it slightly. Add the lamb, stir in the remaining ingredients except the potato, plus half a cup of water and simmer until everything is soft and cohesive. Longer is better than shorter and more tomato paste makes it richer. The mixture should be wet, but not runny. Taste for salt.

Spread evenly over the base of a large casserole dish, spoon the mash on top and run a fork over to leave a ridged pattern. Brush with melted butter. Bake for 20-30 minutes or until lightly coloured.

The simple things are the best. Like butter melting into a crumpet, or the nuttiness and snap of raw asparagus just pulled from the ground. Like a laugh at someone else's expense, undies that don't ride up with wear and beautiful girlie-pink grapefruit juice.

pink grapefruit and campari cocktail
(serves 1)

Pink grapefruit are sweeter than their yellow cousins, but both work well with Campari. As does orange juice, particularly blood orange juice.

juice from 1 pink grapefruit, strained
30ml (1$^1/_2$ tablespoons) Campari

100ml soda water, or for a real thrill try tonic water

Mix all the ingredients together in a tall glass with enough ice to cool it but not dilute it.

I remember the weekend well. It seemed obscene to be writing flippant recipes when diplomacy had been abandoned, and we became aggressors. As I write, we're still at war, so our leaders have failed us. Suffice to say these recipes are pretty easy. As easy as the politics of division.

chinese-style pork ribs with ginger and soy

(serves 4)

1kg pork ribs, Chinese-style (almost as much bone as meat, your butcher should know)

125ml ($^1/_2$ cup) soy sauce

2-3 tablespoons Chinese cooking wine (shaoxing/shao hsing) or use sherry or beer, yes beer

a fat thumb's worth of ginger, finely grated

2 cloves garlic, finely grated or crushed

2-3 teaspoons sugar

cooking time: $1^1/_2$ hours, plus (ideally) 3 to 4 hours marinating

Cut the ribs into manageable sized slabs, say 4 to 5 ribs each. Mix the soy, cooking wine, ginger, garlic and sugar and rub all over the ribs and marinate for a few hours if possible.

Preheat the oven to 150ºC and place the ribs on a tray or two in one layer. Drizzle all the marinade over and add a cup full of water to the tray. Roast for 1 hour, basting every 20 minutes by spooning the cooking liquid from the pan over the ribs. Don't let the tray dry out or the marinade will burn.

After an hour, turn the ribs over and continue roasting and basting until tender, about another half an hour. The trick is to try and reduce the cooking juices onto the meat by basting; the tray should be starting to dry by the time the meat is ready.

Mashed potato. Like socks for the soul. Cheese. The perfect doona-day food. Garlic. Lucky you're not going out. And butter, just because. This French dish is a bit physical to make, but it's kinda fun.

l'aligot

(serves 6)

1kg starchy potatoes, peeled
2-3 cloves garlic, peeled
375ml (1$^1/_2$ cups) milk

150g butter
300g provolone or other mild melting
 cheese, grated

cooking time: 25 minutes

Steam the potatoes with the garlic cloves. When the potatoes are cooked as soft as goose down right through, mash them with the garlic as finely as possible.

Put the milk in a large, heavy-based saucepan and bring to the boil. Vigorously beat in the potato a spoonful at a time with the butter. Turn down the heat and beat until potato is light and fluffy. You can use a hand mixer to do this if it's strong enough, or plop it into the Kitchen Aid.

Sprinkle in the cheese, beating the whole time. The mixture will take on a gloss and come away from the side of the pan as you beat it. It is then that it should be eaten, or left ready to reheat and be eaten.

Serve with just steamed veg or, if you've the constitution, with oven-crisped duck confit, pan-fried Toulouse sausage or some braised smoked ham hock. If there are any leftovers, they're best pan-fried.

Time to remember how impossibly high and blue the sky can be. Time to find an apple with a crunch as big as the tree it's from. Time to fall head over heels. Again. Time to feel that gorgeous giddy feeling when looking into a lover's eyes. It's a melting moment.

melting moments
(makes about 22 biscuits)

180g butter, softened
50g (over $^1/_2$ cup) icing sugar, sifted
good pinch finely grated lemon zest
$^1/_2$ teaspoon vanilla essence

190g (shade over $1^1/_3$ cups) plain flour
60g (just under $^1/_2$ cup) cornflour
$^1/_2$ teaspoon baking powder

cooking time: 15 minutes

Preheat the oven to 180°C.

Beat the butter with the icing sugar, zest and vanilla until light and pale. Sift in the dry ingredients and stir with a wooden spoon until just combined. Roll large teaspoons of the mixture into balls.

Place on non-stick paper on a flat baking tray, far enough apart so they won't touch when cooked (they'll expand a little). Squash lightly with a fork to flatten, leaving a nice pattern. Bake in the centre of the oven for 12-15 minutes or until just lightly browned on the bottom.

While the biscuits are cooling, make the lemon filling. Spread the filling onto half the biscuits and sandwich with the other halves while still soft. Store them in an airtight container.

lemon filling

50g butter, softened
100g (over $^2/_3$ cup) icing sugar, sifted

2 teaspoons finely grated lemon zest
1-2 teaspoons lemon juice

Beat the butter with the icing sugar until smooth, then beat in the zest and juice.

After a night on the tiles, or a day with the blues,
what you need is a little comfort. That's why somebody
invented crumble.

baked rhubarb and apple with pistachio crumble

(serves 6 generously)

200g (1¹/₂ cups) plain flour
120g (²/₃ cup) caster sugar
good pinch salt
120g butter, chilled and diced
100g (about ²/₃ cup) lightly salted
   pistachio kernels, crushed

1 decent sized bunch (500g) rhubarb,
   washed and chopped into 2-3cm lengths
2 apples, cored and chopped
3-4 tablespoons honey
1 teaspoon vanilla essence

cooking time: under 1 hour from thought to dipping in the spoon
you'll also need: a 2 litre, 5cm tall large-based casserole dish or similar

Preheat the oven to 200°C.

Mix the flour, sugar and salt. Rub in the butter with your fingertips (or pulse in a food processor) until it looks nice and crumbly. Add the pistachios and chill for half an hour or so.

Toss the rhubarb and apple with the honey and vanilla (heat honey if it is too thick). Press into the bottom of the casserole dish.

Just before baking, sprinkle the crumble evenly over the fruit, and bake towards the top of the oven for about 30-40 minutes or until the top is browned. Serve with vanilla ice-cream or the raspberry ripple custard, minus the raspberry, on page 178.

Fluff and bubble. With chocolate, which is a bit like love.
With cream, just don't tell your doctor. And with brandy, just
because you bloody well can. Plus you get to lick the spatula.
And run your finger around the bowl.

better-than-body-paint chocolate mousse

(serves 4 to 5)

200g quality dark chocolate or the kind of
   chocolate you like to eat, broken up
30g butter, in small bits
6 eggs at room temperature, separated

125ml ($^1/_2$ cup) cream, lightly whipped
1 tablespoon brandy, Kahlua or
   Tia Maria (optional)

cooking time: 10 minutes to make, a couple of hours to set in the fridge (if you can wait)

Melt the chocolate in a metal or glass bowl over warm (not boiling) water, or in the
microwave on low, stirring regularly. Add the butter and stir to melt in, then remove
from the heat and add the egg yolks. Work quickly from now on.

While the chocolate melts, whip the egg whites to a soft-peak stage – this means that
the egg whites form peaks when you take the whisk out, but the very tips of the peaks
flop over (in theory you should be able to invert the bowl over your head and they won't
slip out, but do this at your own peril, unless you like the egghead look).

Fold one-third of the whites into the chocolate mixture, then fold this mixture into the
remaining whites, until nearly combined. Fold in the cream and the brandy, taking care
not to over-mix. Pop into the fridge to set.

Serve mousse splodged onto the plate with a little more cream.

Today's thinking foodie looks for the flaws. They look for the cake that's risen more on one side because it's homemade. They look for unwaxed apples that haven't spent their whole life in cold storage. And they like to eat shortcake because it tastes better than it looks. And it looks fantastic.

apple and blackberry shortcake
(serves 8 to 10)

200g butter, softened
200g (1 cup) caster sugar
$1/2$ teaspoon vanilla essence
4 eggs
400g (about 3 cups) plain flour
nearly $1/4$ teaspoon baking powder

4 medium-sized Granny Smith apples, peeled, cored, cut into fat slices
80g (more than $1/3$ cup) caster sugar, extra
200g blackberries (frozen are okay)
grated zest from one lemon
50g butter, extra
more caster sugar, for sprinkling

cooking time: 40 minutes, plus an hour to rest between making dough and rolling it
you'll also need: a 24 cm diameter, 4cm deep pie dish, greased and sprinkled with sugar to coat

Beat the butter, sugar and vanilla until pale, then beat in eggs one at a time. It may look curdled but don't worry. Sift flour with baking powder and add to butter mixture, stirring until just combined. Cover and refrigerate 1 hour.

Preheat the oven to 190°C.

Roll two-thirds of the pastry out between layers of plastic film and line the pie dish. Roll out the other third to fit the top, cover and leave in the fridge until ready to assemble.

Toss the apple with the extra sugar, blackberries and zest and fill the pie case. Dot with the extra butter and then top with the reserved rolled out dough. Press edges to seal, cut a slit into the top, and sprinkle the top with a fine dust of caster sugar. Bake in the middle of the oven for about 30-40 minutes. Test with a skewer as you would a cake, and cool before serving with lightly whipped cream, vanilla ice-cream or custard.

Love. As fragile as eggshells. Women. As tender as meringue. Feelings. As easily bruised as stone fruit. Memories. Lightly steeped in vanilla. A good baked custard dish is all those things, and as warming as sheepskin boots. Ugg.

manchester pudding

(serves 4 to 6)

3 slices stale white bread, crust removed
500ml (2 cups) milk
50g ($^1/_4$ cup) sugar
1 tablespoon finely grated lemon zest
20g butter (optional)

4 eggs, separated
100g apricot jam
2 tablespoons sweet sherry or brandy (optional)
1 teaspoon vanilla extract
2 tablespoons caster sugar

cooking time: allow an hour, and time for the pud to cool
you'll also need: a 3-4 litre casserole dish or similar

Preheat the oven to 150°C.

Soak the bread in enough milk to wet thoroughly. When soft, mash to a paste using your hands. Heat this mixture with the remaining milk, add the sugar and zest and boil for 4 minutes. Beat in the butter, allow to cool for 5 minutes, then beat in the egg yolks.

While the milk mixture cools, heat the jam with the sherry, stirring to dissolve, then spread over the base of the casserole dish.

Beat the egg whites with the vanilla and sugar until soft peaks form.

Pour the custard into the casserole dish then carefully dollop the meringue on top. Place the casserole dish in a deep baking tray, and pour in tap-hot (not kettle-hot) water to about 4cm deep around the outside of the dish. Bake for 40-50 minutes or until the custard has set (it's easiest to dig a hole in the centre to test it). If the top starts getting too dark, cover with a lid. Serve at room temperature or slightly warm.

the
busy
weekend

Have you seen my keys? I'm sure I left them on the kitchen bench. Have you got the address, the frozen oranges, the shopping list? The kids, perhaps? I've been loading the car and didn't notice them there. Two big breaths, I'm thinking, to sort the priorities. There may be hair appointments and working bees and family commitments and markets and cafes and church and training, but when you walk back in the door, you'll still want to eat well. Unless you're too busy to care.

Ever wondered how the other half live? I imagine accountants surrounded by dollars. And poets by poetry. I think painters live among rainbows, and lawyers are buried in law, if not justice. Me, I'm busy getting cherry stains on my hands, so I look like a faith healer.

spiced cherries on toasted panettone

(serves 6)

100g ($^1/_2$ cup) sugar
2 pieces cassia bark (or use cinnamon quills)
1 whole nutmeg, cracked into 2 pieces
   (or use a generous pinch of ground)
500g cherries, pitted

50ml ($2^1/_2$ tablespoons) brandy or kirsch
6 thick slices panettone, pandoro or
   raisin bread
250g mascarpone

cooking time: 15 minutes, plus time to cool the cherries

Simmer 125ml ($^1/_2$ cup) water with the sugar, cassia bark and nutmeg for 10 minutes in a covered saucepan. Add the cherries, cover and cook gently for 5 minutes. Remove from the heat and cool, then add the brandy. They keep well in the fridge for weeks.

Toast the panettone under the grill and smear generously with mascarpone. Place on individual serving plates and spoon some cherries and juice over each slice.

Note: This brilliant summertime brunch (or dessert) can be adapted to other seasons. You can substitute any cooked fruit such as poached pear or grilled peach chunks.

Two farmers are having a beer in a pub. The older, wiser, wealthier farmer has been growing tomatoes for 30 years. His mate wants to know which tomatoes to grow to achieve the same success. "Depends," he says, "whether you want to sell the tomatoes, or eat them".

panzanella (tomato and bread salad)

(serves 4)

generous few pinches salt
750g squishily ripe tomatoes, chopped
1 clove garlic, crushed
about 15 basil leaves, torn
250g crusty, stale white bread

1 small red (Spanish) onion, finely diced
80ml ($1/_3$ cup) extra virgin olive oil
freshly milled black pepper
Italian parmesan (or a good, firm sheep's
    milk cheese), shaved with a potato peeler

preparation time: 1 hour, most of it spent picking the kids up from footy

Salt the tomatoes well and leave to stand for an hour with the garlic and basil. It's not essential but it helps.

Tear the bread into smallish pieces. Mash the tomatoes up a bit with your hands and add to the bread with the onion. If it's not wet enough, add more tomatoes, or you could sprinkle in a little water. Tip over the olive oil, and taste for salt and pepper. Top with the parmesan and serve as a small meal or appetiser.

Can't talk. Got to help out at the fundraising barbecue. I know it's the weekend, but there's just no time today. Thanks for the concern, but I'm okay for food. No need to waste money on dodgy fish and chips, I've got pasta, tuna and a lemon in the house.

ten-minute linguini with tuna and lemon

(serves 4)

500g linguini or other long pasta
  (if you're really in a hurry, use spaghettini which cooks in 5 minutes)
200g tinned tuna in oil
2-3 teaspoons finely grated lemon zest

2 teaspoons lemon juice
2 tablespoons chopped flat-leaf parsley (optional)
1-2 tablespoons extra virgin olive oil

cooking time: 10 minutes

Cook the pasta in rapidly boiling, well-salted water until al dente.

While it cooks, open the tuna and break the meat apart with a fork. Don't throw the oil away, for god's sake.

When the pasta is cooked, drain, keeping about 60ml ($1/4$ cup) of the cooking water to toss back on – a quirk of pasta means it gets thirsty just after it's pulled from the water. Splash this water on the pasta then toss it with the tuna and its oil and the remaining ingredients.

Serve immediately, taking care to remember that most of a pasta's garnish will come out of the pot with the last serve, so try to even the tuna out at the end.

The delicate smokiness of fresh water trout. The resolute
nature of spuds. The provocative bitterness of a robust lettuce.
Add it all together and you get a ripper of a lunch.

smoked trout and kipfler salad
(serves 4)

250g kipfler or other good salad potatoes
   or baby potatoes, scrubbed
200g smoked trout fillets (about 4 fillets),
   flaked

2 green (spring) onions, pale parts only,
   finely sliced
2 handfuls well-washed mixed salad leaves
   (try bitter leaves like frisee or radicchio)

cooking time: 20 minutes

Cut the potatoes into 5mm thick slices, or as desired, and plop into a pot of cold water.
Add some salt, bring to the boil and simmer until just cooked through – the slices will take
about 10 minutes or so.

While the potatoes are cooking, make the mustard vinaigrette.

Drain the potatoes well and toss with half the vinaigrette. When they've cooled off a little
(about 5 minutes), add the trout, onion, leaves and remaining vinaigrette, using your
fingertips to toss. Serve immediately.

mustard vinaigrette

2 teaspoons seeded or Dijon mustard
2 tablespoons extra virgin olive oil
juice from $\frac{1}{2}$ lemon, or more to taste
1 small clove garlic, crushed

1 tablespoon chopped fresh herbs (dill is
   good with trout, mixed with other herbs
   like oregano, basil and especially parsley)
decent pinch of sugar

Whisk all the ingredients together well. Keeps well in the fridge.

One pot. One tray. One chance to cook pasta al dente.
One idea. One fabulous vegetarian meal. One thousand
years in the perfecting.

sicilian one-pot penne with broccoli and chilli

(serves 4)

about 1 cup fresh breadcrumbs (optional)
2-3 red chillies, roughly chopped
3 cloves garlic, roughly chopped
500g penne or other short dried pasta
  (it doesn't work with fresh pasta)

1 medium head broccoli, chopped into
  bite-sized pieces
extra virgin olive, oil for drizzling
about 50g grated Italian parmesan

cooking time: 25 minutes

Make breadcrumbs by pulsing stale bread in a food processor until crumbly but not fine like sand. Toast under a grill or in a dry frypan until crisp and starting to brown. Cool.

Bring about 5 litres of water to a rolling boil. The amount of water is important; not 10 litres, not 1 litre, rather use roughly ten times as much water as pasta or you'll not get the same flavour from the other ingredients.

Add the chillies and garlic to the water and simmer for 5 minutes (switch the fan on – the chilli makes you cough). Season the water well with salt and add the penne. Stir so the pasta doesn't stick, bring back to the boil and then add the broccoli. If you want the broccoli crunchier, wait 4 minutes. Cook the pasta until al dente. Drain, add a touch of oil, and place on the table in a big warmed dish.

You dish up the pasta, and everybody dresses their own (strictly in this order, according to my Sicilian friend) with oil, then parmesan and then breadcrumbs.

If this was a nutrition book, the butter would be, well, I don't know but I can't believe it wouldn't be butter. Luckily, this is a weekend book, so you can do all the things you wanted to do all week, like cook steak and eat steak smothered with butter.

minute steak with rocket and mustard butter

(serves 6)

1-2 tablespoons finely shredded washed
   rocket leaf
1 tablespoon horseradish paste
2 teaspoons Dijon mustard
2 tablespoons grated Italian parmesan

40g (about 2 tablespoons) butter, softened
salt and freshly milled black pepper
6 minute steaks, well smashed out
oil, for cooking

cooking time: under 10 minutes

Mix the rocket, horseradish, mustard, parmesan and butter then season liberally with salt and pepper. You can, if you're keen, muddle in a mortar or even chuck it in the food processor.

Season the steaks just before cooking. Heat a pan, barbie or ridged pan until quite hot. Oil the meat lightly and sear on each side for a minute or even less to your tastes. Pop onto warmed plates, smear a little butter paste on each one while it's still hot so it melts quickly.

Serve with boiled new potatoes and some greens if you feel up to vegetables.

Grilled, steamed or even boiled, asparagus is the vegetable that makes spring the season to look forward to. Mixed with a simple nut dressing, you've got a quick, wonderful vegetable dish. Add a fried or poached egg and you've got dinner.

grilled long leg asparagus with crushed hazelnuts

(serves 4)

2 bunches skinny asparagus, tough ends snapped off
1 tablespoon hazelnut, walnut or extra virgin olive oil

salt and freshly milled black pepper
50g hazelnut kernels, roasted and lightly crushed
1 teaspoon lemon juice

cooking time: 5 minutes

Preheat the barbie.

Brush the asparagus with a tiny amount of oil and season with salt and pepper. Grill on the barbie until starting to colour, preferably over coals, but on a hotplate or cooked any way you like will do.

Place the asparagus on a platter and toss the nuts over. Mix the lemon juice with the remaining oil and drizzle over the lot. Serve hot or warm.

According to Eric Bogle, there are three types of people: "sailors", who travel the world looking for its treasures; "dreamers", who dream of sailing abroad to bring home gold; and "schemers", who "take the gold from the sailors and turn it to dross". Weekends are for the first two.

parmesan-crumbed veal

(serves 4)

30g Italian parmesan, finely grated
100g (about 1 cup) breadcrumbs
4 x 120g veal pieces, beaten until thin

plain flour for dusting
1-2 eggs, beaten well
20-40g or more butter, for frying

cooking time: 5 minutes

Mix the parmesan and breadcrumbs together. Dust each piece of veal with flour, dip it into the egg and then roll it in the parmesan and crumb mix.

Heat the butter in a large frypan. Pop in the veal and fry until it is golden on each side, adding more butter if necessary.

Serve accompanied by lemon wedges and the grilled long leg asparagus with crushed hazelnuts on page 60.

Home cooking. Who's got the time in a modern world? With tutors to drop the kids at, bosses to keep happy, emails to-ing and fro-ing, and virtual murders to watch on telly every night. It's easier to open a packet, and if you've no self-respect, you will.

cheesy crunch

(serves 4 to 6 depending on the family)

1kg trimmed lamb chump chops
1 large onion, peeled and sliced thinly
a goodly amount of salt and freshly milled
    black pepper

400g tin chopped tomatoes
about $1/_4$ to $1/_2$ loaf stale white bread
about 200g grated cheddar

cooking time: $2^1/_2$ hours, while you're out
you'll also need: 2-3 litre casserole dish, wide-based rather than taller

Preheat the oven to 180°C.

Lay the chops close together over the base of a casserole dish. Scatter the onion over, season with salt and pepper and pour the tomato evenly across the top. Tear the bread into bits about the size of a man's thumbnail, and chuck over. Rain the cheese on top, cover and bake $1^1/_2$ hours at least so the meat is tender – 2 hours is safer. Take the lid off and cook another 30 or so minutes until the cheese crisps up.

Serve with spuds and make sure everyone gets a chop and some of the topping, or else there'll be fights. Bloody sisters.

Fat juicy oranges. A beach to fill the day. Quick food you can prepare in a caravan. A big coloured towel to sit on. Tan lines. A snorkel. Kids mucking about in a kayak. A light, cooling, fragrant citrus dessert. Must be a weekend away.

spiced oranges with honeyed ricotta

(serves 4)

200g ricotta
40g (2 tablespoons) honey
8 oranges, peeled with a knife
$1/_2$ teaspoon orange blossom water

$1/_4$ teaspoon black pepper
$1/_4$ teaspoon ground cloves
$1/_4$ teaspoon ground cardamom

preparation time: 10 minutes

Whip the ricotta with the honey and refrigerate until ready to use.

Cut oranges into rounds, discarding seeds if you can, reserving juice (or if you know how, segment with a knife). Steep the oranges with the orange blossom water and juice.

Mix the spices together.

Serve the oranges in bowls with a good pinch of spice mixture and a spoonful of ricotta.

If you're after something as quick as a brown fox and as rich as an English Lord, with a good kick from the grog cupboard, syllabub has been invented just for you. It's best, however, made a couple of hours ahead.

syllabub

(serves 6 to 8)

115 g cube sugar (or use loose sugar mixed with 1 teaspoon finely grated lemon zest)
1 lemon, well washed and dried

80ml ($^{1}/_{3}$ cup) sweet sherry
40ml (2 tablespoons) brandy
300ml cream, chilled

preparation time: allow 20 minutes, plus a couple of hours to chill

Rub the cubes over the skin of the lemon to take off as much of the yellow zest as you can. Place the sugar in a bowl, splash over the sherry and brandy and leave for about 15 minutes.

Whisk this mixture in a large bowl until the sugar is nearly dissolved. Whisk in cream, beating until it is the texture of lightly whipped cream. Spoon into serving glasses and chill for at least a couple of hours before serving.

Just because the day has spiralled out of control doesn't mean you can't have dessert. In fact, you deserve it; what with the early morning and the chaos at the shops. This will cook in the time it takes to decide what you're having for dinner.

drunken brown sugar bananas

(serves 1)

1-2 bananas, peeled
melted butter for brushing
1 tablespoon dark brown sugar

about 1 tablespoon rum
(or brandy or whisky)

cooking time: about 15 minutes

Preheat the oven to 200°C.

Slice the bananas in half lengthwise. Place with cut-side down in a baking dish and brush with melted butter. Sprinkle well with sugar and splatter with rum (to 'splatter' rum, partly close the top of the bottle with your thumb).

Bake for 10-15 minutes or until the sugar melts and bananas are soft.

Serve the bananas warm with vanilla ice-cream or cream.

My family, as a way of getting their own back, sometimes buy the ingredients in my weekend recipe columns and generously offer to let me cook lunch. Especially at Christmas. Well I'm going to show them, by serving impressive, simple dishes that taste too good to be this easy.

strawberries with elderflower cream

(serves 4)

300ml pouring cream
60ml (¼ cup) elderflower cordial
  (or use 1-2 teaspoons rose water)

3 tablespoons icing sugar, to taste
3 punnets (750g) strawberries,
  hulled and halved if large

preparation time: 5 minutes

Tip the cream into a big mixing bowl and whisk with the elderflower and sugar until thickening just slightly.

Add the strawberries and gently crush a few with your spoon as you fold them through.

Serve strawberries with a glass of Moscato d'Asti.

You know how you promised to give up a few things in your 40s? Like wasting half the weekend on housework. Like trying to find a use for those preserved lemons you keep getting as presents? Like making dessert from anything but fruit? Well it's weeks and months later so you're allowed butterscotch sauce.

honey roasted figs with butterscotch sauce

(serves 4)

12 fresh figs
about 3 tablespoons honey
130g (²/₃ cup) sugar

40g butter
40ml (2 tablespoons) cream

cooking time: about 15 minutes

Preheat the oven to 200°C.

Place the figs stalk-side up on a lined baking tray and drizzle with honey. Roast about 8-10 minutes or until soft but not completely soggy.

While cooking the figs, heat the sugar in a pan and caramelise over a low flame – it should be browning evenly, but not burning. Cool slightly by placing the pan's base in cold water, then immediately stir in the butter and cream, perhaps warming more to dissolve. (You do run the risk of burning the sugar, or yourself, using this technique, so only do this if you're experienced or are tired of having skin on your hands.) Taste it (once it's cool, dummy) to be sure you haven't overcooked the sugar and turned it bitter.

Serve 3 figs per person, with the warm butterscotch sauce poured over and around, and a dollop of natural yoghurt.

Note: the butterscotch sauce can be tricky for new cooks. If in doubt, add some butter and cream to heated treacle for a different but pleasant sauce.

Okay, so you don't need a recipe to eat raspberries, you just need fingers. But if they're soft and lush and you want a seriously scrummy dessert in minutes, fold them through my version of England's Eton Mess.

not eton mess

(serves 5 to 6)

250ml (1 cup) cream, chilled
2 tablespoons caster sugar
250ml quality vanilla ice-cream, softened
  ever so slightly

handful of crumbled meringue
150g raspberries, more to taste or budget
  (frozen are fine)

preparation time: 5 minutes

Whip the cream with the sugar until soft and moussey.

Fold in spoonfuls of the ice-cream, the meringue and the raspberries.

Serve immediately.

the
romantic
weekend

No, honestly, it's no trouble. Really, I just adore
cooking. I always lay the table, light a hundred
candles and set the stereo on a low groove. I
could take you out for dinner, splashing cash
and showing off, but this is more my style.
Doesn't the room look gorgeous? Like you.
Doesn't the soft glow of candles beat the hell
out of housework? Doesn't the fragrance of the
tipsy cake create a little tingle in your loins?
And don't you remember that a meal shared
was how we courted, all those years ago? Now
put your gear back on and pass me your plate.

If you want to show someone you care, you'll get up before them and make pancakes. You'll sneak around, getting it ready before they've even stretched. If you want to show someone how much you love them, you'll bring them breakfast in bed. Won't you sweetheart? Won't you? WON'T Y... okay, I'll do it myself.

buttermilk pancakes with banana and maple syrup

(makes at least 12 pancakes, but they freeze well)

3 eggs
600ml (nearly 2^1/$_2$ cups) buttermilk
50g butter, melted (or use oil)
2 tablespoons caster sugar
270g (2 cups) self-raising flour (for lighter pancakes, add 1 teaspoon baking powder with the flour)

^{1}/$_2$ teaspoon salt
4 bananas, sliced
200g mascarpone or whipped cream or some butter
plenty of maple syrup, for drizzling

cooking time: 15 minutes

Beat the eggs and add the buttermilk, butter and sugar. Add the sifted flour and salt and whisk until just combined.

Fry the pancakes by spooning a ladle full of mixture in 12cm rounds onto a hot, oiled frypan or griddle (using the ladle's bum to spread the mix if necessary). I use three pans on three burners to speed things up. If not, make sure the cook gets the first one. Turn when bubbles appear on top, and the underside is brown.

Once cooked, keep warm to serve, top with sliced banana and a dollop of mascarpone. Drizzle with syrup and put more on the table for greedy guts. Or use berries and orange curd when in season.

A simple batter becomes crumpets – minus the preservatives you find in commercial versions. Make a whole swag and keep them in the fridge for a couple of days and toast when hungry, or freeze for a while until you next feel like being loved.

crumpets

(makes 25 to 30 tiny ones using egg rings)

750ml (3 cups) milk
1 teaspoon caster sugar
7g (1 sachet) dry yeast

30g butter
500g ($3^2/_3$ cups) plain flour
1 teaspoon salt

cooking time: an hour to rise, an hour to cook (yep, it's a slow process, but quite therapeutic if you like cooking)
you'll also need: egg rings, or even better, bigger, taller crumpet rings

Warm the milk gently so that it feels the same temperature as your finger. Too hot and you'll kill the yeast. Dissolve the yeast in 2 tablespoons of the milk. Dissolve the sugar in the remaining milk and melt in the butter. Mix the flour and salt and stir in the milk and butter then the yeast. Stir until it's an even, fairly thick batter. Cover and leave to rise for about 60-90 minutes in a warmish place. It should be bubbly and able to be poured, though slowly. Transfer to a large jug.

Grease egg rings and a griddle or a large heavy-based frypan. A spray oil works wonders, but butter tastes much better. Heat gently over a medium flame and pour mixture about two-thirds the way up the egg rings. They will continue to rise so don't overfill. Cook for about 6-7 minutes on one side, so the top gets a few holes and has started to dry out, but beware the base doesn't get too dark. A lower heat helps, but too low and the bubbles don't form as well. If they're not forming holes, add a touch more milk to the batter. Remove egg rings, turn over, then cook 2-3 minutes on the other side to brown.

Butter while hot and serve immediately or toast them later for a real treat. Poached eggs are the gentleman's accompaniment.

What is it about a home cooked meal that tells you so much about a person? It can tell you they have an open mind and a heart of gold. It can tell you they have no time for shopping, but time for you. A successful and scrummy end result is just a bonus.

warm haloumi, asparagus and boiled lemon salad

(serves 4)

1 whole lemon
2 teaspoons salt
1 bay leaf
4 tablespoons extra virgin olive oil
1 small clove garlic, crushed

good pinch sugar
250g haloumi (drained and soaked in water if too salty)
2 bunches asparagus, coarse ends discarded, spears cut into 3cm lengths

cooking time: 35 minutes

Juice the lemon and keep 1 tablespoon for this dish, the rest for later. Pop the juiced halves in a small saucepan, cover with water, bring to the boil, add salt and bay leaf and simmer 30 minutes or less until soft. Drain and cut away the pulp and discard. Finely dice the skin and combine with the lemon juice, 2 tablespoons of the olive oil, the garlic and sugar.

Slice the haloumi into bite-sized slices 5mm thick, and fry in enough olive oil to brown properly. Drain and keep warm.

Blanch the asparagus in boiling water for just a minute, then drain and toss with the haloumi and dressing. Serve with lots of Turkish-style bread.

In my mind, the weekend is more than just another scrub of the tub and whip around with the Dyson. It has a different sentiment altogether, like big swings hanging from trees and streams where kids linger with yabby nets. I saw it painted on a café table in Mildura: jump in the river with me and kiss me underwater.

grilled iceberg with prosciutto and gorgonzola

(serves 4 as an appetiser)

1 small tight head iceberg or
   cos lettuce, outer leaves removed,
   heart cut into quarters
1-2 tablespoons extra virgin olive oil

8 thin slices prosciutto
200g gorgonzola dolce or other creamy
   blue cheese

cooking time: 5 minutes

Remove the lettuce from the fridge 15 minutes before you want to eat. Heat a char-grill or ridged pan until really hot. Sear the cut sides of the lettuce hearts very briefly on the grill until coloured.

Serve each lettuce heart with a drizzle of olive oil, 2 slices of the prosciutto and a knob of the blue cheese.

You're in a caravan near a lake. You're on a promise and the food is really just something sensuous to refuel before more kissing. What you really want is good, honest food that cooks reasonably quickly. And you want the recipe now.

superfast penne with buffalo mozzarella and tomato

(serves 2)

2 soft, ripe tomatoes, hulled and chopped
100g buffalo mozzarella, cut into bite-sized
    pieces (you can also use fresh bocconcini,
    ricotta or goat's cheese, with lesser results)
1 tablespoon extra virgin olive oil,
    plus more, for drizzling

5 basil leaves, torn into bits
salt and freshly milled black pepper
250g good-quality dried penne
grated Italian parmesan, for serving
    (optional)

cooking time: 12 minutes

Mix together the tomatoes, mozzarella, olive oil and basil and season well with salt and pepper, tossing to combine.

Cook the penne in heavily salted boiling water until al dente. Drain, reserving 2-3 tablespoons of the cooking water. Tip the pasta back into the hot cooking pot with the reserved cooking water, and stir well, then quickly toss in the tomato mixture and mix well.

Serve immediately with more pepper, oil and parmesan.

Just because you're cooking for two, doesn't mean you can't be making meals to enjoy during the week. If this dish doesn't get you some brownie points, maybe you need a new girlfriend.

braised chicken with peas and tarragon

(serves 5 to 6)

100g butter
1 large (about no. 20) chicken, jointed
  (or equivalent bits)
1 large onion, peeled and diced
500ml (2 cups) white wine

2-3 tablespoons fresh French tarragon leaves
salt and freshly milled black pepper
300g peas (frozen are fine)
100g risoni (rice-shaped pasta)

cooking time: 1 hour

Heat the butter in a large, preferably cast-iron saucepan over a low flame and gently brown the chicken. Drain and remove. In the same pan, fry the onion until soft, but try not to brown it. Return the chicken to the pan, pour in the wine and sprinkle in half the tarragon.

Turn up the heat and boil vigorously for 5 minutes or until the wine has lost its strong alcoholic smell. Add about 250ml (1 cup) water and bring to the boil again. Turn down, cover and simmer for about 45 minutes (you can do this in an oven). At this point, season with salt and pepper. Tip in the peas (they can be straight from the freezer) and risoni. Only thing to watch is that there's enough liquid. The risoni will double in size, absorbing it's own weight in water, so it should be fine so long as you haven't boiled the buggery out of the chicken before. If there's not enough liquid, add another 125ml ($^1/_2$ cup) water. Stir as the mixture comes back to the boil to stop the risoni sticking.

Cook until the risoni is tender, add the remaining tarragon. Check for salt and pepper again, then serve with bread and a lightly oaked chardonnay.

Always pretty, scallops on the half shell are probably the easiest, most impressive entrée dish to cook a prospective partner. Even raw they're edible (and desirable as sushi). Just don't overcook them or you might blow it.

steamed scallops with ginger and green onion
(serves 2)

12 scallops on the half shell,
  loosened from shell
1 green onion, trimmed and cut into
  fine slivers

2cm ginger, peeled and cut into
  fine shreds
2 red chillies, cut into 12 fine slices
soy sauce, for drizzling

cooking time: 2 minutes

Place the scallops in a bamboo or other steamer, on the shell. Overlap shells if need be, but be sure the meat is exposed. Pop some green onion, ginger and 1 or 2 slices of chilli on top of each one and steam for about 2 minutes or until they've changed colour but haven't shrunk and overcooked.

If you don't have a big bamboo steamer, place scallops on plates, cover with foil and bake for 5 minutes or so at 200°C.

Place on a serving plate, reserving all the juice in the shell, and drizzle each with a little soy.

If I was trying to seduce someone, I know what I'd do. I wouldn't be super fancy. I wouldn't take all day and still run the risk of it not working out. But I would take the time to revisit mash.

hot smoked salmon with crushed horseradish spuds

(serves 2)

300g waxy potatoes (try kipfler, dutch
    cream or pink eyes), peeled and steamed
50g butter
salt and freshly milled black pepper
1 tablespoon creamed horseradish paste
1 green (spring) onion, finely sliced

200g hot smoked salmon (you can also use
    fish or sear your own fresh salmon if you
    can't find the hot smoked stuff), cut into
    two pieces and perhaps warmed
1 tablespoon baby capers
1 tablespoon chopped fresh dill

cooking time: 10 minutes

While the potatoes are still hot, toss into a bowl, add the butter and crush a bit with the back of a spoon. Add salt and pepper to taste.

Fold through the horseradish and onion and dollop onto plates. Top with smoked salmon and serve with capers and chopped dill.

Eyes like smoky candles. The clink of crystal. The flicker of passion, of firelight on sandstone. The prick of lemon juice, of a conscience. Pond-like calmness, seen on the surface of a sacher torte. Thin, tight lips, like a clam. Then dinner, at last.

slow-roasted rib-eye rubbed with porcini and mustard

(serves at least 4)

2kg beef rib-eye, on the bone with
  about 4 ribs
$1/_2$ cup seeded mustard

3 tablespoons porcini powder (optional)
3 tablespoons olive oil
3 teaspoons salt

cooking time: 1 hour to stand, $1^1/_4$ hours to cook (rare) and 15 minutes to rest

Trim the rib-eye if needed and score the fat. Mix the mustard, porcini powder, olive oil and salt and rub well all over the outside of the meat. Allow to stand for about an hour at room temperature.

Preheat the oven to 250°C (or use any brand of kettle style barbecue).

Roast the meat for 15 minutes at 250°C, then turn the oven right down to 110°C (take care, some ovens switch off around this temperature, and others' thermostats aren't very reliable – my stupidly expensive Gaggenau is brilliant). Cook for about another hour for quite a pink meat. Crank the oven again for a bit to make sure the outside is nice and hot, then rest under foil for 15 minutes before carving.

Note: Porcini powder, a cheaper alternative to slices of dried porcini, is sold in some delis. Failing that, puree soaked dried porcini, or just use mustard and it'll still taste grand.

Like a bank with compassion and understanding. Like having an opportunity for true reconciliation, but not having a true statesman. Like having a kiss without tenderness. Some things just don't seem right. But some dishes just do.

stir-fried prawns with snake beans and lemongrass

(serves 2 to 3)

2 tablespoons peanut or vegetable oil
10 snake beans, cut into 3 cm lengths
2 stems lemongrass, pale part only, very finely diced (use a food processor if need be)
5cm piece ginger, minced or grated
4 small green chillies, finely sliced

400g green prawns, de-veined, tails kept on for better presentation
3-4 tablespoons coconut cream
juice from $1/2$ lime
1-2 teaspoons palm sugar, grated, to taste
1 tablespoon fish sauce, to taste
15 fresh basil leaves, washed

cooking time: 5 minutes once you heat the wok

Heat the oil in a wok until quite hot, add the snake beans and toss well. Add lemongrass, ginger and chillies and fry another minute without letting them colour too much. Toss in the prawns and stir-fry until they change colour.

Add the coconut cream, lime juice, sugar and fish sauce to taste. Remove from the heat then toss in the basil leaves. Serve immediately with steamed rice.

If you really want to impress someone, especially the person you've been living with for the past 20 years, an excellent vegetable dish could be just the ticket.

just yummy peas

(serves 4 to 6 as a vegie)

30g butter
1 small onion, peeled and finely chopped
4 slices prosciutto or equivalent jamón
  or ham

500g frozen baby peas
salt and freshly milled black pepper

cooking time: 5 minutes

Heat the butter and fry the onion until soft. Add the prosciutto and cook 2 minutes longer. Tip in the peas and occasionally stir gently as they cook (the water should come from the peas as they thaw) in just a few minutes.

Season to taste (the prosciutto will have added some salt) and serve.

front: just yummy peas; back: gorgeously simple broad bean and parmesan salad

If you want to show that important soul what they really mean, you won't take them out. You'll do the rarest of deeds, and the simplest. Double peel some broad beans and if they don't love you more than ever, you're with the wrong person.

gorgeously simple broad bean and parmesan salad

(serves 4)

300g double peeled cooked broad beans (frozen will work okay, but fresh are better), warmed if desired
1 tablespoon fresh lemon juice

2 tablespoons extra virgin olive oil
4-5 fresh basil leaves, finely shredded
salt and freshly milled black pepper
40-60g Italian parmesan, finely grated

preparation time: 10 minutes

Toss the beans with the lemon juice, olive oil, basil, salt and pepper and lay in a serving dish. Sprinkle generously with parmesan.

Serve salad with crusty bread.

Anybody who loves a drink should adore you if you make them a little cocktail to kick off the night. Using the sparkling trill of limes, the deep, Jamaican accent of golden rum and the crisp harmony of mint, chances are you're in.

mojito
(serves 1)

¹/₄ lime, cut in half again
2 tablespoons caster sugar
50ml good-quality golden rum

10 mint leaves, well washed
crushed ice
soda or mineral water, for diluting

Use a solid rod to muddle and crush the lime and sugar in a sturdy container.
Tip into a cocktail shaker, add the rum, mint leaves, some crushed ice and shake well.

Pour into a whisky glass and fill with soda water.

I don't need to wait until Valentine's Day. I don't need a Hallmark moment as an excuse to show someone I care. And I don't need a love in my life to have crepes for brunch. But unless you can eat a lot of crepes, it doesn't hurt to have company once in a while.

sugared lemon crepes
(makes 16 to 20 crepes)

4 eggs
2 tablespoons sugar
500ml (2 cups) milk
180g (1¹/₃ cups) plain flour, sifted

1 tablespoon lemon zest, finely grated
40g butter, melted
caster sugar, for sprinkling
lemon wedges, for squeezing

cooking time: make the batter 30 minutes before using, then it's 10 minutes to cook

In a bowl or food processor beat the eggs, add the sugar and milk then whisk in the flour. Sieve if lumpy. Add the zest and butter and rest for 30 minutes.

To cook, ladle a little batter into a hot, lightly buttered crepe or non-stick frypan, and swirl to evenly coat the pan. When brown on one side, turn over and cook the other side a few seconds. Continue until they're all cooked.

Sprinkle each crepe with a little sugar, roll them tightly, four to a serve. Sprinkle with a little more sugar then warm under a grill or in the oven just before serving. Squeeze heaps of lemon over and serve with a glass of Grand Marnier.

Note: if the crepes are too thin and hard to turn, whisk a little extra flour into the batter to help them firm up.

Billawarra yoghurt. A pinch on the bum. Someone to wash up. Pork crackling, a little private dance as you wait for the vegetables to cook. Freshly squeezed orange juice. A stolen kiss, tipsy cake and fingers licked. Makes the kitchen the best room in the house.

tipsy cake with orange blossom mascarpone

(serves 3 to 4)

250g mascarpone
60g ($^1/_2$ cup) icing sugar
2 teaspoons orange blossom water
   (or try Grand Marnier)
zest and juice from 1 orange

2 eggs, separated
125ml sweet sherry or try brandy
roughly 12 savoiardi biscuits
about 50g dark chocolate, grated

preparation time: allow 20 minutes plus 3-4 hours to set in the fridge
you'll also need: a 1 litre serving bowl or individual serving dishes

Mix the mascarpone with 2 tablespoons icing sugar, the orange blossom water, 1 teaspoon orange zest, 2 tablespoons orange juice and the egg yolks. Whisk the egg whites with another 2 tablespoons icing sugar until soft peaks form. Fold a quarter of the whites through the mascarpone mix to lighten, then fold in the remaining whites, until just combined.

Whisk the remaining orange juice with the sherry and remaining icing sugar in a bowl to dissolve. Soak each biscuit in this liquid, placing immediately in the bottom of a serving bowl or individual dishes – use half the biscuits like this. Top with half the mascarpone mixture, then repeat with the remaining soaked biscuits (mixing up more of the liquid if you run out) and finishing with the remaining mascarpone.

Refrigerate for 3-4 hours at least, before serving topped with the grated chocolate.

There's magic to be found nearby. Like eating a piece of soft fruit from the nape of a lover's neck. Like the paper, draped all over the house as if you're about to start painting, when all you're doing is reading. And like a recipe that never goes out of style.

lightly bitter orange jelly with orange salad

(serves 4 to 6)

rind of 1 orange
100g sugar
600ml water
2 teaspoons gelatine
6 oranges (use those fantastic coloured blood oranges if available), peeled and segmented, including any juice

1 tablespoon icing sugar
2 whole star anise
2 whole cloves
few drops orange blossom water (optional)

cooking time: 5 minutes, allow a few hours for jelly to set and overnight for salad to infuse
you'll also need: use 100ml glasses or containers to hold the jelly

Using the blunt end of a wooden spoon (if you have a mortar and pestle, use that), mash the rind with the sugar to release the fragrant oils. You don't smash it up, just press the rind firmly, using the sugar for friction.

Heat the water with the sugar and the rind in a saucepan until it simmers. The longer you cook it, the more bitterness will come from the skin, so take care not to overdo it. Whisk in the gelatine, stirring well to dissolve. Strain into individual dishes and refrigerate until set.

For the salad, mix the oranges with the icing sugar and spices, stirring to distribute the sugar. Add the blossom water and leave overnight, or for a few hours at least, to steep. Serve with the jelly on the side.

Note: the jelly isn't strong enough to be moulded, rather it is soft and gentle on the lips.

The Saturday morning ritual. Flesh against flesh. A cuddle to start the day. Later it'll be ice-cream as sensual as a reclining nude. A frozen dessert as sweet as a sleep-in. What you want is silken and yielding, but with a residual firmness.

banana, brown sugar and sour cream ice-cream

(serves 8 to 10)

500g ripe bananas
4 eggs, separated
2 teaspoons lemon juice
100g (about $^2/_3$ cup) dark brown sugar

300g sour cream, whisked smooth
100g (about 4 tablespoons) glucose syrup
 (sometimes called corn syrup)
pinch salt

cooking time: under half an hour to make, but 4 hours to freeze

Peel the bananas and plop the flesh into the bowl of a food processor. Whiz it up with the egg yolks, lemon juice and sugar until smooth. Stir into the sour cream, then mix until silky (or you could pulse in the sour cream in the food processor).

Whisk the egg whites with the glucose and salt until soft peaks form. Gently fold a quarter of the egg white into the banana stuff until nearly combined. Fold this lightened mixture into the remaining egg whites until an even consistency. Put into an ice-cream container and freeze for at least 3-4 hours. Like all ice-cream, once firmly frozen it's better if moved from the freezer to the fridge for 20 minutes before serving.

the
social
weekend

Of course we must. Having Baz and Scooter
and Maggot and Tonk over, with all their tribes,
is what weekends are for. You name the time,
because I'm offering breakfast, lunch or dinner.
We may fire up the barbie, or pot roast a chook
or just drink elderflower and gin drinks. Or
we may serve lettuce cups filled with prawns.
I'll pull out the placemats and the good glasses,
the tea cosy and the well worn old jokes. Any
way it happens, this is the weekend to catch up.
We really must.

Let's face it, if someone is dropping by unexpectedly for breakfast, they've probably arrived late the night before and decided not to chew their arm off. Burritos are fancy enough to look like you've planned days ahead when you haven't.

scrambled egg burritos with bean salsa

(serves 2)

200g cooked white beans or try butter beans (tinned are fine), rinsed well
1 green (spring) onion, finely sliced
$1/_2$ clove garlic, crushed
1 ripe tomato, diced
2 teaspoons white wine vinegar
1 small red chilli, finely diced

1 tablespoon extra virgin olive oil
salt and freshly milled black pepper
4 tortillas
4 eggs, seasoned and beaten with a fork
20g (about 2 tablespoons) gruyère, emmenthal or other mild cheese, grated

cooking time: allow 20 minutes cooking plus 30 minutes standing time

Drain the beans well and mix with the onion, garlic, tomato, vinegar, chilli and half the olive oil. Season with salt and pepper, and leave to sit at room temperature for 15-30 minutes if possible.

Preheat the grill.

Heat the tortillas according to the instructions on the packet. Heat the remaining oil in a frypan and cook the eggs with half the cheese as if making scrambled eggs, but don't let them become too firm. Lay the tortillas on the bench, place a quarter of the egg on each one and roll up. Top with the remaining grated cheese and grill until the cheese melts.

Serve two for each person, with the bean salsa on the side.

If I were in charge, I'd encourage home cooks to believe in themselves because ingredients, like dogs, can smell fear. I'd want the afterlife to include biscuits from a battered old tin, and loaves of bread baked in a woodfired oven. I'd have time for a big, leisurely brunch every weekend. And I'd leave my friends just as they are.

sweet corn fritters

(serves 6)

This recipe is adapted from one Josie Chapman cooked at The Old Convent near Orange, in rural NSW.

4 fresh corn cobs
1 red capsicum, finely diced
6 green (spring) onions, finely sliced
1/3 cup chopped fresh herbs such as dill, basil and oregano
1/3 cup chopped fresh flat-leaf parsley
135g (about 1 cup) self-raising flour
1 dessertspoon sugar

1 teaspoon each salt and freshly milled black pepper
1 teaspoon smoky paprika (optional, or use normal paprika)
2 eggs
125ml (1/2 cup) milk
sunflower oil, for frying

cooking time: a bit of chopping, plus 10 minutes cooking

Cut the corn kernels from the cobs and discard the core. Mix the corn, capsicum, onion and herbs.

Sift together the flour, sugar, salt, pepper and paprika. Whisk the eggs, add the milk then add to the flour mixture. Stir to combine and just bring together, then add to the vegetables. Mix lightly until just hanging together. Always stir lightly before scooping as the batter tends to drop out to the bottom of the bowl.

To cook, heat 2 tablespoons of oil in a large frypan over a medium to low heat. Scoop in heaped tablespoons of mixture in batches and allow to flatten out. Fry to golden brown on one side, turn and cook the second side until brown.

Serve immediately for brunch with a salad, roasted tomato and goat's cheese.

After I've thrown the sudoku page down in frustration, it's the freezer's turn to get a freshen up. There's a bag of peas. And chunky leg ham hiding behind the vodka bottle. The visitors are coming in 45 minutes. One-pot meal, here we come. After a vodka and tonic, of course.

summer pea and ham soup
(serves 6)

80g butter
1 leek, paler parts only, washed and
  finely chopped
200g ham, finely diced
400g (2 cups) risotto rice

3 litres chicken stock
salt and freshly milled black pepper
400g frozen baby peas
100g Italian parmesan, finely grated

cooking time: about 30 minutes

Heat the butter in a large saucepan and fry the leek gently, so you hear a faint hiss from the pan. Use a wooden paddle to move it around occasionally and continue frying until the leek is soft but not browned, about 5 minutes.

Add the ham and rice, then drown the lot in the stock and add seasonings (remember the ham will furnish the broth with some salt, and so will the parmesan at the end).

Bring to a boil then turn right down to a gurgle. Stir occasionally until the rice is cooked through, about 15-20 minutes. It will depend on the brand. Tip in the peas and bring back to the boil. Remove from the heat and stir in the parmesan. Leave it to sit a couple of minutes while you get the bowls and plates ready and call out "dinner". Serve hot.

Duck. The new brown meat. All it takes is an oven and some time, and you'll snare one of the finest flavours known to man. Tossed through a salad, it's easy to look like a cook when all you've been doing is having fun mucking about in the kitchen.

shredded duck salad

(serves 4 as part of a meal)

2 roasted duck legs, warmed, flesh stripped from the bone and shredded with your fingers
about $1/4$ small red (Spanish) onion, finely sliced
a couple of radishes, finely sliced
two good handfuls torn, mixed lettuce leaves

20ml (1 tablespoon) sherry or other flavoursome vinegar, even balsamic
40ml (2 tablespoons) walnut oil or extra virgin olive oil
about $1/4$ teaspoon salt and some freshly milled black pepper

preparation time: 10 minutes if duck legs are already cooked

Mix the duck with the onion and radish and toss to combine, then mix with the lettuce leaves and gently distribute with your fingers.

Whisk the sherry, oil, salt and pepper until well combined.

Dress the salad, toss with your fingertips and serve immediately.

The duck's skin can be cut, salted and crisped in a pan and added to the salad at the last minute. It's kind of like duck crackling.

Note: roasting duck, particularly the marylands (legs) is easy. Bung in a 180°C oven with a little salt and pepper, skin-side up, and cook for over an hour, or until so tender you can shake the meat from the bone. Roast a whole heap and use the leftovers to make a salad.

Some things are best done outside. Some things are funny and irreverent, and also taste good. Some recipes just seem to suit our lifestyle. And when it's beer o'clock and there's a chook to roast, this recipe, of dubious origins, is an absolute crack up.

up-the-duff chook
(serves 4)

1 tinny beer
1 x no. 16 chicken, rinsed and patted dry
about 10 sage leaves (this is just being fancy)

olive oil, for rubbing
salt and freshly milled black pepper

cooking time: allow an hour
you'll also need: a barbie with a lid

Preheat the barbie.

Swig down half the can of beer. It's important. Push sage leaves under the skin of the chicken over the breast using your index finger. Rub a little olive oil over the bird with your hands to coat evenly, then season well, inside and out, with plenty of salt and pepper.

Hold the beer can upright on the bench, then impale the chicken with it, so the tinny is standing upright, and the chicken is sticking up in the air, legs facing down. Pick the whole lot up keeping it the same way up, and place the tinny on the hotplate. What happens is that the beer will steam the inside of the bird while the outside browns.

Cover and roast for 30-40 minutes. Check by inserting a knife in the joint between the leg and breast to make sure it's no longer pink.

Rest a few minutes, take great care removing the beer can (it may still have boiling beer in it), hack the chicken into four and serve.

Yep. That's right mate. A barbie, at my place. Bring the littlies. We're going to cook pizza on the chargrill. Show off the new courtyard. You make your own pizza, so it doesn't matter how late you mob are.

pizza cooked on the barbie

(makes 2 to 3 pizze to feed 2 to 3 people)

1 recipe pizza dough (see page 126)
extra virgin olive oil
sugo or other good-flavoured fresh
   tomato puree
thinly sliced toppings such as mushrooms,
   tomatoes, prosciutto, artichokes, olives

buffalo mozzarella (allow 1 ball per pizza
   if you're generous), or other cheeses
fresh herbs especially fresh basil, rocket
   and oregano
salt and freshly milled black pepper
finely grated Italian parmesan

cooking time: under 10 minutes once rolled out
you'll also need: pizza trays and a barbecue, preferably with a lid (otherwise you'll need a big heatproof bowl to cover your pizza trays leaving at least 2cm extra around the sides)

Preheat the barbecue with the lid down.

Let each person make their own pizza. Roll out the dough thinly, using a mist of flour and stretching it with your hands until it's the size you want and lay on a pizza tray. Brush with enough olive oil to make it glisten. Dot with barely-there toppings, say nothing more than a few wafer thin slices of tomato, then tear the buffalo mozzarella and basil into pieces and dot around.

Season with salt and pepper, scatter with a vague hail storm of parmesan then roast, lid down, on the chargrill if you have one, checking every 2 minutes. It will scorch on the bottom, not so much on top. Turn and move it to a cooler part if starts to become too dark.

Chunks of basic bread dough can be rolled thin (under 1cm) with fresh rosemary, then brushed with good olive oil and chargrilled. Turn over when coloured and serve with hummus (see page 136), or use it to make superb pizze as shown on previous page.

pizza dough
(makes enough for 2 to 3 pizze)

270g (2 cups) plain flour
7g (1 sachet) dried yeast
1 teaspoon salt

1 teaspoon sugar
olive oil, for drizzling

preparation time: 10 minutes, and best made a day or two ahead

Mix the dry ingredients together. Make a well in the centre and pour in 200ml (a tad over $3/4$ cup) tepid water, mix with a spoon, then finish with your hand to make a smooth-ish dough.

Form into a ball, rub with olive oil, pop into a bowl big enough to let it expand and cover with plastic film. Keep in the fridge; 2 hours is okay, 2 days is best.

Note: made a day or two ahead, something happens to a bread dough and its gluten to ensure it requires virtually no kneading.

According to a Chinese saying, if a man wants to be happy for a week, he takes a wife. If he wants to be happy for a month, he kills a pig. And if he wants to be happy for a lifetime, he plants a garden. At some point I think he may also learn how to cook.

porchetta

(roast pork scented with garlic, fennel and rosemary)

(serves 6)

1.5kg pork loin, boneless, rind removed
2 cloves garlic, crushed
3 sprigs fresh rosemary
2 teaspoons fennel seeds

2 tablespoons chopped fresh
   flat-leaf parsley (optional)
salt and freshly milled black pepper

cooking time: a bit over an hour cooking, plus 15 minutes resting
you'll also need: string for tying, or ask your butcher for one of those nets they use

Preheat the oven to 200°C (or light the barbie).

Open the meat to the flesh side. In a mortar (or food processor) mangle the garlic, leaves from 1 sprig of rosemary, fennel seeds, parsley and about 1-2 tablespoons salt plus some pepper. Smear this all over the inside of the loin and then roll up and tie tightly, slipping the remaining two pieces of rosemary under the string to flavour the outside. Sprinkle the outside with bit more salt and pepper.

Roast in the oven, on the spit or in an enclosed barbecue for one hour or until just cooked – you can serve pork pink in Australia now, and that's not a bad thing. Take from the oven, cover with foil and wait about 15-20 minutes before slicing and serving. The scraps are really yummy reheated, too.

Yes, seriously, you can cook a soufflé. The twice-cooked soufflé is much more resilient than the other kind, and you can prepare it ahead so it's great if you're of having people over but don't want to risk doing a new recipe on the day.

twice-baked gruyère soufflé

(makes 6)

60g butter
50g (shade over 1/3 cup) plain flour
250ml (1 cup) milk
60g finely grated gruyère
1 tablespoon finely grated Italian parmesan

salt and freshly milled black pepper
3 eggs, separated
about 200ml cream
extra grated gruyère, for serving

cooking time: 40 minutes, but make them ahead
you'll also need: six 200ml heatproof ramekins or moulds and 6 heatproof serving dishes

Grease moulds and preheat the oven to 180°C.

Make a super-thick white sauce by melting the butter in a saucepan, adding all the flour and cooking over a gentle heat for 1 minute, stirring constantly. Add the milk a little at a time, whisking until smooth. Simmer for 1 minute on the lowest flame. Stir in the cheeses and enough salt and pepper so it tastes great. Allow to cool until you can touch it without burning your fingers then beat in the egg yolks.

Beat the egg whites with a pinch of salt until they reach the soft peak stage and fold into the cheese mixture. Gently spoon into your buttered moulds and place in a baking tray with deep sides. Fill the tray with enough hot water to come about one-third the way up the sides of the moulds and bake for 15-20 minutes or until set. Remove from the oven and cool.

At serving time, preheat the oven to 180C again.

Unmould the soufflés and place upsidedown on individual heatproof serving dishes. Tip 1-2 tablespoons cream over each one, top with extra gruyère, and bake until the cheese starts to colour, about 10-15 minutes. Place on serving plates so you don't scorch the table.

You know how we've said we must catch up. Well, we will. Instead of fighting the crowds for yum cha, why don't you come over for a textural marvel? You'll get messy hands, the heady flavour of prawns and a big, glossy lipped grin.

prawn sang choi bao
(serves 4 as a starter or as part of a meal)

1 firm-ish iceberg lettuce, outside leaves discarded
1-2 tablespoons peanut or other oil
1 tablespoon young ginger, finely chopped or grated
250g green prawn meat, chopped (from about 600g whole prawns)
2 tender young celery sticks, chopped finely
230g tin water chestnuts, chopped

4 (about 15g) dried shiitake mushrooms, soaked in 2 tablespoons hot water, drained, stems discarded, tops finely sliced
1 tablespoon Chinese cooking wine (shaoxing/shao hsing), or dry sherry
2 tablespoons oyster sauce
1 teaspoon sesame oil
4 green (spring) onions, sliced finely
handful lightly crushed salted peanuts

time: about half an hour to prepare, 2-3 minutes to cook

Hit the core of the lettuce firmly against the bench and twist to remove. Slice 1cm off the lettuce at the opening. Under running water, gently separate leaves, one at a time, keeping them whole to use as lettuce "cups". Soak in cold water for 30 minutes to crisp. Drain and pat dry.

Heat the oil in a wok over the biggest flame you have and stir-fry ginger for 30 seconds. Toss in the prawn meat and stir-fry until about half cooked – it will still look slightly glassy. Throw in the celery, water chestnuts, mushrooms and their water and stir to heat through. Put in the wine, oyster sauce and sesame oil and onion, give it a good toss and stir while the sauce coats the other ingredients and thickens a little.

Tip into a serving bowl and sprinkle on the nuts. Put on the table next to the lettuce. Each person half fills a lettuce cup then folds the lettuce in and chomps down. Be sure to have some serviettes for mopping up gloriously sticky fingers.

132

Rain on a hot tin roof. The smell of salt in the air and the hair. The intoxicating perfume of peaches and dinner dates. Lemon on peas. These are the scents of days off.

pan-fried lemon whiting with crushed peas

(serves 4)

300g peas (frozen are fine)
40g butter
salt and freshly milled black pepper
$1/_2$ teaspoon finely grated lemon zest

4 large whiting fillets
butter, for frying
fresh lemon juice, for squeezing

cooking time: 10 minutes

Simmer the peas until tender and mash gently with the butter, some salt, pepper and the lemon zest.

Season the whiting and fry in melted butter until just changed colour inside. It should take less than a minute on each side. Lay fish over the peas.

Reheat the whiting pan (add a little more butter if dry) until the butter goes a nut-brown colour. Squeeze in some lemon juice and tip this over the fish and peas.

Go on. Light the barbie. Invite a few friends around and tell them not to bring any meat. But do drop a hint that a salad of sliced tomato with red onion and sumac and a drizzle of olive oil would be awfully nice.

lightly herbed lamb cutlets with hummus

(serves 4 and makes a generous amount of hummus)

$^1/_4$ cup washed coriander leaves, finely chopped
$^1/_4$ cup washed mint leaves, finely chopped
finely grated zest and juice from $^1/_2$ lemon

$^1/_4$ teaspoon ground cumin
salt and freshly milled black pepper
enough extra virgin olive oil, to moisten
12 small lamb cutlets

cooking time: 5 minutes for the lamb plus overnight marinating, and 2+ hours for the hummus

Mix everything except lamb to make a rough paste. Rub all over the lamb and marinate overnight if possible. Grill on a preheated barbie about 2 minutes each side or until cooked the way you like. Serve with hummus.

hummus

200g dried chickpeas (tinned won't do it justice), soaked overnight, rinsed
1 onion, halved
2 bay leaves
4-5 cloves garlic

1 tablespoon tahini (sesame seed paste)
2-3 tablespoons extra virgin olive oil
2-3 tablespoons fresh lemon juice, to taste
1 teaspoon salt
$^1/_4$ teaspoon ground cumin

Put the chickpeas in a big pan with 1 litre of water, the onion and bay leaves. Simmer, covered, for 1-2 hours or until very soft, checking that the liquid stays above the chickpeas. Drain, keep the cooking liquid but discard the bay leaves and onion. Process the garlic then add some still-hot chickpeas. Puree with the remaining ingredients in batches, taking care not to overload the food processor and adding some cooking liquid for a smooth paste. Mix in a big bowl with a little pepper to taste, then cool.

Legs. The things to stand on while making carrot sticks for guests. Thighs. Something we hope don't get the texture of bush lemons. Wings. A band that Paul McCartney formed after The Beatles. Breasts. The first tender months of life. Cider. Something that makes the rest even more attractive.

pot-roasted cider chicken with speck and baby carrots

(serves 4)

a drizzle of olive oil
150g speck or pancetta, chopped
1 large red (Spanish) onion, chopped
about 5 cloves garlic, bruised
2-3 fresh bay leaves

16 or so baby carrots, peeled and
  ends trimmed
375ml ($1^1/_2$ cups) dry apple cider
  (or try wheat beer)
1 x no. 16 chook

cooking time: a bit over 1 hour

Preheat the oven to 180°C and taste the cider.

Heat the olive oil in a big ovenproof pan, preferably cast-iron or similar, with a tight fitting lid. Fry the speck until it starts to sizzle. Add the onion, garlic and bay leaves and fry to gently brown the onion.

Add the carrots, pour in the cider and boil rapidly for 2 minutes. Add the chicken, breast-side down, and cover. Place in the oven and cook for 30 minutes while you open a fresh bottle of cider to check the quality. Taste the chicken sauce for seasoning (the speck is salty, so you may not need too much), turn the chicken over and cook for another 30 minutes or so without a lid, so the skin can colour and the sauce reduces a bit. In the meantime, chat earnestly about politics or tell a few gags while you imbibe another bottle or two of cider.

Skim most of the fat off the top of the sauce. Rest a few minutes (the chicken, silly, you've already been resting for an hour) before cutting the bird to serve with a sharply dressed salad, some boiled buttered chats and a glath or two of that thcrumptiouth thider.

Some food tastes better than it should. It's too easy, too delicious, too bloody good for the effort. Other things are a shopping nightmare, but fantastically simple once you've found the right supplier. This elderflower drink is one of the latter, though supermarkets have recently started stocking this aromatic liquid.

elderflower, gin and soda refresher

(serves 1)

ice cubes
1 tablespoon elderflower cordial
  (available from good food stores)

1 tablespoon gin
about 200ml soda water

Mix a little ice with the other ingredients in a tall glass and sip at lunchtime, preferably outside and with shorts and thongs on.

Oh, and if you happen to forget the gin, it's nearly as nice.

Grower's market for cheese? Done. Casual invite for the mob to come over for tea. Done. Real biscuits that don't have trans fats, a bad aftertaste or a bad attitude? Done like dinner. Which I've got to get done too. Better get cracking…

gingernuts
(makes about 14 large biscuits)

250g (about 1³/₄ cups) plain flour
60g (3 tablespoons) caster sugar
1 teaspoon baking powder
2 teaspoons ground ginger

¹/₄ teaspoon mixed spice
100g butter, chilled and diced finely
¹/₃ cup treacle or golden syrup

cooking time: 20 minutes in total

Preheat the oven to 180°C.

Mix all the dry ingredients in a bowl (or use a food processor). Rub butter into the dry ingredients until it looks crumbly (or pulse in a food processor). Tip in the syrup and knead to make a stiff dough.

Roll into balls a bit bigger than the diameter of a 50-cent piece. Press onto a lined baking tray so they're reasonably flat, about 7-8cm wide. Bake for 10 minutes or until starting to colour nicely. Cool and store in an airtight container.

A tea cosy. A floral plate. A visitor is expected.
Better make biscuits.

chunky almond biscuits

(makes 35 to 40 biscuits)

125g butter, softened
135g (1 cup) caster sugar
1 egg
180g (1$^1/_3$ cups) plain flour
$^1/_2$ teaspoon ground ginger
$^1/_2$ teaspoon ground nutmeg

$^1/_2$ teaspoon baking powder
$^1/_2$ teaspoon salt
125g unblanched whole almonds
40 (about 50g) extra unblanched whole
   almonds, for garnishing

cooking time: 20 minutes total

Preheat the oven to 180°C.

Cream the butter and sugar until pale. Beat in the egg. Mix the flour with the spices, baking powder and salt then fold into the butter mixture. Blitz the 125g almonds in a food processor until a fine yet crumbly texture. A few chunks are fine. Fold into the biscuit mixture.

Line two trays with baking paper or silicone sheets and dot with about 1 tablespoon of mixture at regular intervals, leaving enough space for them to spread a little. Press a whole almond into the top of each one and bake about 8-10 minutes or until they start to tan up nicely. Remove from the oven and cool well before storing in an airtight container.

front: chunky almond biscuits; back: gingernuts

Anybody who bakes usually has a regular stream of guests dropping by "for a cuppa". Once they've tried this you may have to clear out the spare room. It's worth the effort to make your own pastry.

pecan and golden syrup tart

(serves 6 to 8)

1 recipe sweet shortcrust pastry (see below)
75g butter
20g (about 1 tablespoon) sugar

2 tablespoons golden syrup
40ml (2 tablespoons) pouring cream
250g pecan kernels, lightly broken

cooking time: 30 minutes if the pastry is baked, otherwise 90 minutes from start to finish
you'll also need: a 20cm flan tin or similar, with a removable base

Preheat the oven to 200°C. Line the greased flan tin with the shortcrust pastry, freeze for 30 minutes then bake blind until the base is cooked. Reduce the oven to 180°C.

Heat the butter, sugar, syrup and cream in a large saucepan and simmer for 1 minute. Fold through the nuts and spread evenly over the prepared pastry case.

Bake at 180°C for about 25-30 minutes or until the top starts to colour (take care the edges of the tart don't colour too much – you can cover them with foil if need be). Cool well in the tin before removing. Store in an airtight container and serve at room temperature.

sweet shortcrust pastry

100g butter, softened slightly
90g icing sugar, sifted
$1/2$ teaspoon vanilla essence

1 teaspoon lemon zest, finely grated
170g ($1^1/_4$ cups) plain flour, sifted
1 egg yolk

In a food processor process the butter with the icing sugar, vanilla and zest until dissolved. Pulse in the flour until the mixture is crumbly then add the egg and pulse. Tip the mix onto the bench and knead just until it makes a dough, adding a dribble of water if it's too dry. Refrigerate for 30 minutes before rolling between sheets of plastic film.

There's something fabulous about a crowd pleasing pudding that isn't trying too hard to be fashionable. Shiny clear orbs of sago are given the South-East Asian treatment, and go down a treat on a warm day.

sago pudding with coconut cream and palm sugar caramel

(serves 4)

100g sago
1-2 teaspoons caster sugar
a pinch of salt

50g palm sugar, grated, if needed
1-2 tablespoons water
200-300ml (about 1 cup) coconut cream

cooking time: 15 minutes, plus 15 minutes standing

Bring 2 litres of water to a rapid boil, add the sago, stir and simmer for 15 minutes. Cover with a tight lid, and let stand 15-20 minutes or until the sago is completely translucent. Strain, cover the sago with cold water and rinse well. Drain.

Heat the caster sugar with a tiny little bit of water to dissolve. When dissolved, add a pinch of salt and tip onto the sago. Leave in the fridge until ready to serve.

To make the caramel, heat the palm sugar in a saucepan until it goes a deep golden colour. Tip in the water (careful, it may spit) and stir over the heat until it forms a liquid. Cool before serving.

Serve the sago with some coconut cream around, and drizzle over some palm sugar caramel.

An open fire. A dog at your side. The wind rustling through the cantankerous gum trees outside and a fine-leaved old recipe book in your hands. These are all very good things. When they come with company, it's even better.

steamed treacle pudding
(serves 6 to 8)

60g butter, softened
200g (1 cup) caster sugar
1 egg

135g (1 cup) self-raising flour
250ml (1 cup) milk
3 tablespoons treacle or golden syrup

cooking time: 2 hours
you'll also need: a 2 litre pudding tin or heatproof basin, plus a lidded saucepan to fit it in

Cream the butter and sugar until pale — it will stay crumbly, but don't worry. Beat in the egg, then the flour and the milk in two batches. Grease and flour a pudding tin and pour the treacle into the bottom. Tip in the pudding batter and seal the lid. (If you don't have a pudding tin, use a heatproof bowl and cover the top with plastic film and then foil, then tie tightly underneath the rim to seal and tie a handle across the top too.)

Place the pudding tin in a large saucepan. Pour in hot water until one-third of the way up the tin. Bring to a simmer, cover the saucepan with a tight fitting lid and steam for about 2 hours, checking occasionally that there's enough water in the pan.

Very gingerly remove the pudding tin from the water, take the lid off and run a knife around the tin if needed. Tip the pud onto a plate and serve warm with jersey cream (if you can).

Want a cool dessert? Something made the day ahead to pull out and impress the dinner party crowd? An iced treat with the lushness of white chocolate, rum and the restrained power of spice? Well you probably want a slice of parfait.

white chocolate and rum parfait

(serves 6 to 8)

5 eggs, separated
100g ($^1/_2$ cup) caster sugar
1 teaspoon vanilla essence
2 tablespoons rum
300ml thickened cream

40g (about 2 tablespoons) honey
100g white chocolate, broken and very gently melted
1 teaspoon ground allspice (or use mixed spice if you don't have allspice)

preparation time: 20 minutes to mix, overnight to freeze

In a sparkling clean bowl, with clean beaters, whisk the egg whites with half the sugar until soft peaks form. That's when the mix holds itself up, but the ends of the peaks flop over when you pull out the whisk.

Whisk the egg yolks with remaining sugar, vanilla and rum until pale and thick.

Next, whisk the cream until reasonably thick and moussey.

Stir the honey, white chocolate and spices into the egg yolk mixture until even. Fold in the cream, then a quarter of the egg whites. When lightened, fold in the remaining egg whites. Mix only until just smooth, taking care not to knock out too much air. Freeze in a 2 litre rectangular container until firm (perhaps lined with plastic for easy removal).

Take from the tin when frozen and serve slices with whatever poached fruit is in season.

the slow

weekend

Can you pass the gardening book please. Aaaaauuuwhh. No, not yawning, stretching. Killing time while the beans soften. The curry cooks. The pork sozzles in beer. This is the weekend for laying in and getting someone to cook you pancakes. Slow enough for risotto – in bed. It's time for properly cooked polenta, or lamb so tender it cuts with a coarse accent. The slow weekend is a time for simmering soups and engrossing novels and sowing seeds and teaching the kids to draw. It's a weekend of nanna naps and refining your iTunes playlist, of podding peas and long luxurious baths. Midweek it seems these weekends come around terribly slowly.

On a Saturday, you might think there's a pelican's nest in the hair, but everybody's doing it in Milan. And no-one can be blamed for thinking my strides look remarkably like tracky daks. It's not that I'm avoiding the washing up – I just can't start anything domestic until I'm well fuelled up for the day.

apple and cinnamon breakfast risotto

(serves 4 to 6)

1 litre milk
1 vanilla bean, split lengthways
   (or use 2 teaspoons vanilla essence)
3 strips lemon peel taken with
   a potato peeler
100g (about $1/_2$ cup) caster sugar

125g (about $2/_3$ cup) arborio or
   other risotto rice
2 Granny Smith apples, peeled,
   cored and diced
good pinch ground cinnamon

cooking time: 30 minutes, better if made an hour ahead

Heat the milk, vanilla bean, lemon peel and sugar in a decent sized saucepan. Add the rice and stir every few minutes as it simmers for about 20 minutes or so. Stir in the apple and the cinnamon. Keep simmering, stirring occasionally, until the rice is very soft – about another 10 minutes. It will thicken up as it cools. Remove the vanilla bean and lemon peel and let it stand for about an hour or so.

Serve warm or at room temperature with some more fruit, such as baked rhubarb, if you want.

A cooler morning. The lure of the pillow. A late night followed by a really late breakfast. Sounds like it's time to break out the hash browns because it's so hard to get good ones when you go out for brunch.

hash browns with fat sliced speck, spinach and egg

(serves 4)

400g speck in a chunk, rind removed
400g unpeeled starchy potato
  (white rather than yellow fleshed ones)
$^1/_2$ small red (Spanish) onion, peeled and finely diced
1 teaspoon chopped fresh thyme (optional)

about $^1/_2$ teaspoon salt and some freshly milled black pepper
about 20g butter
200g cooked spinach, tossed with butter
4 poached or fried eggs

cooking time: 1 hour if you use speck, less if you just fry bacon

Steam the speck for an hour or until tender. Cut into four and sear in a hot, oiled pan to crisp the outside.

In the meantime, scrub and steam the potatoes whole until they're nearly cooked, but retain some firmness. Rinse with cool water so you can hold them and use a knife to rub off the skin. It's best to do it while the potatoes are still warm.

Grate the potato coarsely and mix well with the onion, thyme, salt and pepper.

Heat the butter gently in a non-stick frypan. Using your hands, divide the potato mixture into four and form balls. Gently squash into the frypan to make four flat disks. Cook the potato well, until deep brown on one side, then turn and cook the other side, adding just a touch more butter if you want. Serve warm with the speck, spinach and eggs.

Note: the trick with hash browns is getting the potato to stick together. Par cooking changes the starch's character.

156

Last weekend, I told myself I'd be good. There were gutters to clean and friends to call. So I borrowed a kilo of flour and made currant rolls and pancakes, and then ate them all without sharing with the neighbour who provided the starch. Maybe this week I'll be more inclusive.

blueberry pancakes with apple butter
(serves 2)

1 apple, peeled and cored
1 tablespoon sugar
100g butter, softened
ground nutmeg or cinnamon (optional)
1 egg
125g fresh ricotta
100ml (more than $1/_3$ cup) milk

20ml (1 tablespoon) vegetable oil
1 tablespoon caster sugar
90g ($2/_3$ cup) self-raising flour
$1/_2$ teaspoon baking powder
$1/_4$ teaspoon salt
about 200g blueberries (frozen are fine)
butter or oil, for frying

cooking time: 25 minutes

Cut the apple into bite-sized chunks and stew with a tiny dribble of water for about 10-15 minutes, with the lid on, until soft. Add the sugar and mash to a pulp. Cool, then beat into the butter. Perhaps flavour with a little nutmeg or cinnamon.

While the apple is cooking, beat the egg and ricotta. Add the milk, oil and sugar. Add the sifted flour, baking powder and salt and stir until just combined – if the mixture is too stiff, add a little more milk so it forms a thickish pancake batter. Fold in the blueberries.

Fry the pancakes by spooning a ladle full of mixture in 12-15cm rounds onto a medium-hot, buttered frypan or even better, the very clean hotplate of a barbecue. Use the ladle to spread the mix if need be. Turn when bubbles appear on top, and the underside is brown. Once cooked, keep warm, and serve 2 or 3 per person with a dollop of apple butter on top.

Soaking. Something it's good to do to beans. And soaking is also great to do in the bath. I adore weekends because there's time to do things like soak beans and cook beans and eat beans and have a long luxurious lounge in the tub. It's been a while.

borlotti bean and spinach soup

(serves 3 to 4)

This recipe epitomises the Italian phrase *brutta ma buona* – ugly but good – thanks to brown beans. Beans vary in cooking time, so always allow more time than a recipe says, just in case.

250g dried borlotti beans (the stripy ones),
  soaked overnight if possible
4 cloves garlic
1 onion, peeled
2 good healthy sprigs fresh sage
1 sprig fresh rosemary
big handful fresh flat-leaf parsley,
  roughly chopped

1 bunch English spinach, well washed,
  stalks discarded and leaves chopped
  (or use frozen)
1-2 extra cloves garlic, crushed (optional)
a goodly amount of extra virgin olive oil
salt and freshly milled black pepper

cooking time: usually up to 2 hours

Run the bath. Meanwhile, heat the borlotti beans with 1.5 litres of water, the whole garlic cloves (don't bother peeling them), the onion, sage and rosemary. Bring to a boil then simmer for 1-2 hours or until cooked through. The beans should be tender enough to mash. Keep an eye on the water level so the beans stay covered.

When you've towelled off, go back to the stove, fish out the onion and the garlic, plus the herbs if you can find them (the leaves fall off). Use a stick blender to quickly pulse a few times. The idea is to rough up some of the beans, but not all, into a paste. Don't make a smooth puree. Stir in the parsley and spinach and simmer another 10 minutes, topping up with more water if need be, so it's soupy and not overly thick. Add the extra garlic towards the end of the cooking (for a hotter, pungent flavour) or earlier if you want it milder. Drizzle in some olive oil, I'd use a good 2 tablespoons, and taste for salt and pepper.

160

Beans. As humble as a shoe and as noble as a Tuscan lord. The source of angst in Jack's house until he proved their worth. A wonderful food sometimes best indulged in when you're sleeping alone. A big pot of slow-cooked beans, however, is best shared.

tuscan-style slow-braised beans with red wine and sage

(serves 6)

2 cups dried white beans (northern or cannellini), soaked overnight if possible
400g ripe tomatoes, chopped, or use tinned
1 prosciutto, bacon or ham bone, a chunk of speck or ham hock to your liking
400ml (over $1^1/_2$ cups) red wine

2 sprigs fresh sage
1 sprig fresh rosemary
2 cloves garlic, peeled
2-3 tablespoons extra virgin olive oil
salt and freshly milled black pepper

cooking time: several hours in the oven

Cover the beans with plenty of fresh water and simmer for 1 hour. Drain and place in a large ovenproof dish that has a lid.

Add the tomato, bone, wine, sage, rosemary and garlic to dish. If the dish is flameproof, heat again on the stove, adding 500ml (2 cups) of water. The beans should be covered with liquid. Add the oil, cover the pan with the lid, and place in a preheated warm oven (120°C or so, just check your oven doesn't switch off at low temperatures – some do) and cook for 1 hour. Remove the lid, stir to make sure it's not sticking, add salt to taste and some pepper. Cover, place back in the oven and cook for another couple of hours, checking occasionally. I switched the oven off and left the beans to soften overnight. The idea is to make them as tender as a lover's sigh, without boiling them rapidly so they fall apart.

Serve with real bruschetta – bread grilled rather than toasted, preferably over coals – and drizzled with *una croce*, a cross, of fine extra virgin olive oil.

Ricotta gnocchi are delicate, slightly rich dumplings that can be paired with a hint of any pasta-style sauce (though tomato-based cut the cheesiness nicely). Real ricotta, drained in a colander and sold fresh at delis, is much better than the stuff supermarkets sell.

ricotta gnocchi
(serves 4)

500g ricotta
1 egg
100g grated Italian parmesan
  (a tangy cheddar also works)

salt and freshly milled black pepper
100g ($^3/_4$ cup) plain flour
more plain flour, for rolling

cooking time: 5 minutes to mix, 10 minutes to roll and 5 minutes to cook

Mix the ricotta, egg and parmesan well. Taste for salt and pepper and fold in the flour until evenly distributed – don't overwork or it can become gluey. You can do this a few hours ahead, and it's better if you do – just be sure to refrigerate the ricotta mixture while you do other things.

When ready to cook, take a wide-based pan and bring plenty of well-salted water to the boil. Take a teaspoon of mixture at a time and roll into balls, using flour on the outside to prevent it sticking. When you have them all rolled, pop the balls into the simmering water and cook until they float to the surface. This cooking is important. Don't jiggle the pan or stir it. Don't nudge the gnocchi to make them rise to the top. It will only take a few minutes, though you may have to do it in two batches.

Remove them as they rise to the surface using a slotted spoon, dabbing the bottom on a cloth as you do so. Place directly onto serving plates.

Serve hot, perhaps with browned sage butter over the top (very rich), or with a little tomato cooked with onion and olive oil, finished with a handful of rocket wilted in at the end.

In parts of Italy, huge pillowy mounds of slow-cooked golden gruel are spread onto large boards, topped with ragu and placed in the centre of the table. Family members mark out their territory, eating from the outside in. Tradition dictates that you should cook over a wood fire and only stir the polenta in one direction. As if.

soft polenta with mushroom ragu

(serves at least 6)

2 teaspoons salt
350g (2 cups) polenta

100g butter
100g ($1^2/_3$ cups) finely grated Italian parmesan

cooking time: allow over an hour for the polenta and 20 minutes for the ragu

Heat 2 litres of water until nearly boiling then add the salt and sprinkle in the polenta, stirring constantly. Bring to the boil then turn down and simmer very gently. Stir often, using a flat-bottomed wooden spatula, for at least 40 minutes though an hour is even better. I stir every few minutes, keeping a lid on in-between to stop it splattering. If it becomes hard to stir, add a little more water. Fold in the butter and cheese until melted and taste for seasoning. Serve immediately with mushroom ragu.

mushroom ragu

60g butter
3 large onions, peeled and diced
2-3 cloves garlic, crushed
1kg large flat mushrooms, diced

salt
375 ml ($1^1/_2$ cups) red wine
600g crushed tomatoes (tinned are fine)
good grind freshly milled black pepper

Heat the butter and fry the onions until soft, add the garlic and give it another minute. Toss in the mushrooms and some salt and fry as well as you can until they soften right down. Add the wine, boil until nearly dry, then stir in the tomatoes and pepper and boil down until thick and rich. Add some sage or basil for flavour if you like.

Friends told me of their favourite soup, as old as our nation, as warm as a cuddle, as comfortable to slide into as an old jumper. I didn't steal my friends' recipe. That way I'll also have something to look forward to at their place.

lamb shank and pearl barley soup

(serves 6 to 8)

about 1 tablespoon butter or olive oil
2 large onions, chopped
2 large carrots, chopped
$1/4$ bunch celery, chopped
2 bay leaves

4 lamb shanks
few sprigs fresh thyme (a pinch dried will work fine)
4 handfuls (about 150g) pearl barley
salt and freshly milled black pepper

cooking time: $2^1/_2$ hours – though if you want to take the meat from the bone, it can take a while to cool enough to handle

Heat the butter in a large heavy-based saucepan that has a tight fitting lid until it is right hot, lad. Cast-iron is perfect. Fry the onions, carrots, celery and bay leaves until tender, but don't brown them. Add the shanks and enough water to cover (about 2-3 litres is usual). Bring to the boil and skim off all the fat and stuff that comes to the surface. Add the thyme and barley, cover and turn right down (or pop into a low oven) for about 2 hours or until the meat falls easily from the shanks.

Skim again to remove any excess fat that will have risen to the surface. Remove the shanks carefully with tongs and allow to cool enough to handle them. Take the meat from the bones, discard the bones and cut the meat into bite-sized pieces. Return to the pan, add salt and pepper to taste, and bring back to the boil. Simmer another 20 minutes to meld the flavours even more.

Serve the soup in the biggest bowls you have, with slices of buttered bread, on days when you want to feel loved.

The trick with a good curry often lies with flavourings – especially fresh "herbs" such as onion, ginger and garlic. In this curry they have to be gently browned by slow cooking. The longer and slower the better. And as usual with curry, this one's best the next day.

indian-style beef, brown onion and cardamom curry

(serves 4 to 5)

1-2 tablespoons vegetable oil or ghee
1 kg beef shanks, cut osso buco-style
  by the butcher (or try goat)
2 large onions, finely sliced
fat thumb of ginger, grated
3 cloves garlic, crushed or grated
1 cinnamon stick

1-2 small dried red chillies
5 brown cardamom pods
  (or 20 smaller green ones)
1 teaspoon ground cumin
$1/_2$ teaspoon ground coriander
1 large tomato, chopped (or 200g tinned)
salt and freshly milled black pepper

cooking time: 2 hours

Heat some oil in a large pot over a medium flame and fry the meat until it goes a good tan colour. You may need to do this in two batches. Remove and keep to one side.

In the same pan, possibly adding more oil, fry the onion very slowly until it starts to colour. I like to add a bit of salt while it fries to draw out moisture. Add the ginger and garlic and keep frying, stirring often, until it all goes a glorious light brown colour. It may stick a bit, which is fine, just scrape the base of the pan with a wooden spatula if it looks like it may burn.

Add the cinnamon, chillies and cardamom pods, stir and fry until it becomes fragrant – about another 2 minutes. Stir in the cumin and coriander and fry another 30 seconds. Throw in the tomato, return the meat to the pan, and add roughly 500ml (2 cups) water, enough water to barely cover. Stir to rub off any stuck bits from the bottom. Season with salt and pepper, put a lid on and cook for about $1^1/_2$ hours or until the meat falls from the bone. You can do this in the oven if you like, but if you do it on the stove, stir occasionally to avoid it scorching on the bottom. Serve with steamed basmati rice, pappadums and cucumber raita.

Anything that warms the house is a good thing in the cooler months. If you make a big pot of this, freeze the leftovers, and you can warm the soul anytime.

three pork and bean stew
(serves 8 to 10)

olive oil for frying
150g speck or pancetta, skin removed
  and cut into 2cm cubes
800g pork neck meat, cut into large dice
2 coarsely ground pork sausages
2 onions, peeled and diced
2 carrots, peeled and diced

2 celery sticks, diced
2 bay leaves
375g lima beans or other dried cooking
  beans, soaked overnight if possible
400g tin chopped tomatoes or
  equivalent fresh
salt and freshly milled black pepper

cooking time: 2 hours

Heat 2 teaspoons or so of oil in the base of a large saucepan and fry the speck to release some fat. Then fry the pork and sausages to brown well, perhaps in two batches depending on the size of the base of your pot. Remove the meats with a slotted spoon.

In the same oil, gently fry the onions, carrots, and celery for a few minutes to soften. Cut the sausages into bite-sized bits, tip the meats back into the pot, add the bay leaves, beans, tomatoes and 2 litres of water. Bring to the boil, skim, turn right down and simmer for 70-90 minutes or until the beans are soft. Season well with salt and pepper and cook another 10 minutes, adding more water if necessary to make a stew consistency.

Serve alone or with bread, with a healthy amount of salad to follow.

Beer for breakfast? Even on a Saturday it's an aberration. Three ten-litre kegs perch like drunks at the kitchen table and we're slurping them on a very fresh palate. It's amazing how you can get a taste for something. So the pork will get sozzled slowly in it for a couple of hours. Sounds strangely familiar.

wheat beer sozzled pork spare ribs with sage and garlic
(serves 4)

2 stubbies wheat beer (or use other beers preferably that aren't too bitter)
1kg pork spare ribs, 2cm thick
2 medium potatoes, peeled and cut into modest chunks (or use whole scrubbed baby potatoes, 300-400g)
2 large green onions, cut into pieces the length of your last thumb joint

2 medium carrots, peeled and cut into batons the length of the onion
6-7 cloves garlic, peeled and maybe roughly chopped
big handful sage leaves
$1^1/_2$ teaspoons salt and some freshly milled black pepper

cooking time: about 2 hours

Put the oven on 200°C. Have a swig of beer.

Pull the pork out of its bag and check it over. If it looks gritty, give it a rinse. Get the baking or roasting tray (or even a wide casserole) and lay the pork on the bottom in one layer. Push the potato between the meat so it will be covered with beer. Scatter the onions, carrots, garlic and sage over. Sprinkle evenly with the salt then tip the beers all over. You want the meat to be just about submerged, maybe fully submerged but not by much. If you need more liquid (I did just say have one swig of beer) use water. If there's too much beer pause now while you imbibe.

Cover the tray with foil and pop it into the oven. Cook for 1 hour. Take the foil off and cook another 30 minutes so the top of the pork starts to colour and poke above the sauce. Turn the meat and cook another 30 minutes (try laying the meat on top of the vegies for best effect). You want the pork to look browned but not burnt and the sauce moist but not overly runny (add a touch of water if it dries out). Serve immediately from the oven.

Long time no see. The pot roast came and went and came again. Pot roasting keeps things tender and moist, and holds in all the flavour. To celebrate the slow weekend, I've used a whole leg of lamb, though you could try shoulder too.

four-hour olive and lemon scented leg of lamb

(serves 4 to 6)

You could use the same paste on a roast, but this tastes even better if you've got the time.

1 medium-sized leg of lamb
about 10 fleshy black olives, pitted
about 6 cloves garlic, peeled
5-6 slices lemon

3 bay leaves
$1/_2$ onion, diced
125ml ($1/_2$ cup) red wine
salt and freshly milled black pepper

cooking time: the clue is in the recipe name

Preheat the oven to 150°C. Take the lamb from the fridge about half an hour prior to cooking, if possible.

Blend or pound the olives with the garlic until a coarse paste is formed, adding a little water if necessary. Smear all over the lamb, particularly the fleshy bit that will face upwards. Place in a large sealable pot (you can use a tray and foil, or even an oven bag, but a pot is best). Lay the lemon slices over the lamb, and the bay leaves. Put the onion, wine and 125ml ($1/_2$ cup) water in the base of the pan and season the leg well with salt and pepper. Don't forget, however, that the olives will probably already be salty. Put the lid on, pop in the oven, turn down to about 110°C and cook for 3-4 hours, checking on occasion that the pan hasn't dried out. Add a splash more water if it does. It should get more juices that drip from the lamb.

Serve the very tender meat with baked potatoes in their jackets and a bowl full of peas.

There are some things it's probably better not to make public, like the fact you think feng shui is a crock, or you've paid $8 for a punnet of berries. Or the fact you've made a fish soup that isn't authentic. As long as it tastes marvellous.

cheat's bouillabaisse

(serves 4)

2 tablespoons olive oil
1 leek, paler parts only, washed well and finely chopped
1 fennel bulb, peeled if necessary and finely shredded (if you can't find fresh fennel plop in 2 star anise with the tomatoes)
2-3 cloves garlic, crushed
good pinch saffron threads (the quantity relies somewhat on the generosity of the cook, but don't use turmeric)

650g super-ripe fresh tomatoes, skinned and chopped, or equivalent tinned
1 teaspoon salt
250ml (1 cup) decent white wine
1 bay leaf
freshly milled black pepper
12 live mussels (not green-lipped ones), de-bearded
400g fish fillets, such as red mullet and snapper, cut into 2 cm cubes

cooking time: 25 minutes

Heat the oil in a large saucepan and fry the leek and fennel very slowly until they lose their crunch. A lid helps. Add the garlic and saffron and cook another minute. Toss in the tomatoes and fry until almost dry, stirring constantly. Add salt, wine and bay leaf and boil rapidly for a minute. Add 1 litre or so of water. Simmer for 10 minutes, season with pepper, then add the mussels. When they open, add the fish. Bring back to a simmer, remove from the stove.

Serve immediately with garlic-brushed croutons or olive bread and a good semillon.

Cranberries, an international company says, grow on you. I'm sure. So does a k.d. lang and Tony Bennett CD. And so does ear hair and tinea. None of which mean that I have to like them. But I do like to think, that if more people ate more custard, the world would be a more peaceful place.

raspberry ripple custard
(serves 6)

1 litre milk (full cream, unless you've got no self-respect)
3 tablespoons wheaten cornflour (if using pure corn cornflour, use 5 tablespoons)

2 teaspoons vanilla essence
8 egg yolks (or use 5 eggs)
130g ($2/_3$ cup) sugar
100g raspberries (frozen are fine), warmed until they just start to fall apart

cooking time: 5 minutes to make, 10 minutes to cool

Use 3 tablespoons milk to dissolve the cornflour in a large bowl. Heat the remaining milk until nearly boiling. Whisk vanilla, eggs and sugar into the cornflour mixture until smooth. Whisk the hot milk into the egg mixture. Return to the stove in a clean pan and bring back to the boil, whisking constantly, to thicken.

Allow custard to cool a bit then fold through the raspberry mixture until you get a lovely ripple effect. In the stone fruit season, serve with peaches or nectarines or on its own at any time. And in winter, fold through cooked rhubarb instead of the raspberries.

I blame cafés. Nobody comes over on the weekend for afternoon tea, or afternoon caffe lattes or afternoon sticky topped yoghurt cake. If only they knew what we'd been baking.

yoghurt cake with lemon syrup
(serves 8 to 10)

125g butter, softened
200g (1 cup) caster sugar
3 eggs
zest and strained juice of $1/_2$ lemon
200g ($1^1/_2$ cups) self-raising flour

200g ($3/_4$ cup) natural yoghurt
80ml ($1/_3$ cup) water
150g ($3/_4$ cup) sugar
lightly whipped cream, for serving

cooking time: allow over an hour until it comes from the oven, but eat the cake cool
you'll also need: a lined 20cm cake tin

Preheat the oven to 180°C.

Cream the butter and sugar until pale and light. Beat in the eggs, one at a time. It may look a bit curdled but don't worry, we'll fix that. Fold in the lemon zest and flour gently and then fold in the yoghurt too. Use a spatula to scrape into the cake tin, making the centre a little lower compared to the edges. Bake for about 30-40 minutes or until a skewer comes out clean.

While the cake is cooking, heat the water, sugar and lemon juice in a small saucepan and simmer for 5 minutes. When the cake is cooked, leave it in the tin, poke a fine skewer into the cake all over about 30 times and spoon the hot lemon syrup over the top. Try to spoon it so it soaks into the holes evenly rather than all soaking into the edges around the tin. Allow to cool in the tin.

Serve with cream, coffee and a grin.

Nothing speaks of a slow weekend like an old-fashioned pud. Take the time to zest lemons, to whisk eggs, to tell everybody that today's the day you're making lemon delicious. And watch how slowly time seems to pass until the pudding is ready.

lemon delicious

(serves 2 to 6, depending on sweet tooths)

This is adapted from a recipe given to me by Pat O'Donnell, who also cooks the world's best golden syrup dumplings. I've published that recipe so many times that it may be going to her head.

50g butter, softened
130g (²/₃ cup) caster sugar
4 tablespoons plain flour, sifted
pinch of salt

grated zest and juice of 4 lemons
500ml (2 cups) milk
4 eggs, separated

cooking time: about 1 hour total
you'll also need: a 2 litre, 7cm tall casserole dish

Preheat the oven to 180°C.

Beat the butter and sugar and fold in the flour and salt. Fold in the lemon zest and juice and stir the milk through (the mixture should be quite runny). Fold through the egg yolks.

Whip the egg whites to snow (I love that old-fashioned term). Fold in a quarter of the egg white to lighten the lemon mix, then fold in the remainder.

Pour into a greased casserole dish then place the dish in a tray. Pour in enough hot water to come two-thirds of the way up the pudding's sides (this is more than for most recipes). Bake for about 40-50 minutes, or until the top is golden. Allow to cool for half an hour before serving (it will sag as though it's disconsolate, but that's perfectly normal, and it's really quite a cheery dish).

Serve with loads of vanilla ice-cream.

acknowledgements

I'd like to express my gratitude to the team at *Good Weekend*, especially editor Judith Whelan, for publishing the original Weekend Cook column. To Tim Whiting and Jill Brown at Random House, thanks once again for the opportunity to put out a lush cookbook and your tremendous support while doing it at such short notice. To the rest of the team, including the talented designer Mel Feddersen, it was a joy to work with people interested in highlighting the yum-factor.

To Jody Vassallo, all credit to you for managing me, and us, and them, to get the book out in a tight time frame and doing it with such grace and warmth. Working without a food stylist meant a huge learning curve and a super-sized thank you must go to Jane Hann for her calm guidance and exquisite props. I'm indebted to Marie-Helene Clauzon for letting me raid the French plates in her garage, to Sally Webb for allowing the Limoges porcelain out of the house, and to Ros Muirhead for those quirky yet fantastic cloths, dishes and aprons we found stashed in the sideboard. Thanks also to Nick Haddow for lending me his marvellous brass ladle.

In the kitchen, it's a big hooray to Alice Storey and Samantha Joel for cooking for photography while I spent way too much time looking through the camera. Thanks to Annie Nutter and Maureen Rowe for the almond biscuit recipe, which I've adapted from the one they hand wrote for me. Thanks also to Suzy Peters for the pizza technique. Huge gratitude to the Anderson family for showing me how to steam a chook over a beer can; for the wine that lubricated many a dish (and the cook); and for the wonderfully pungent olive oil, which I'll miss when this last batch is gone. Oh, and for bringing up a terrific daughter who shares my life.

To photographer and friend Alan Benson: see, we can work together and still be talking a month later. The book looks beautiful thanks to you. I'm in awe of your talent and appreciate the supreme extra effort and patience you put into this project.

And finally to Megan Anderson, who cooked, criticised, cajoled and cuddled me during the best and worst of it. This book attempts to honour my love of our weekends spent together.

Matthew Evans

index

Random House Australia Pty Ltd
Level 3, 100 Pacific Highway, North Sydney, NSW 2060
www.randomhouse.com.au

Sydney   New York   Toronto
London   Auckland   Johannesburg

First published by Random House Australia 2007

Evans, Matthew, 1966–.
         The weekend cook.
         ISBN 978 1 74166 584 0 (pbk.).
         1. Cookery. I. Title.
         641.5

Cover and internal photography by Alan Benson
Cover and internal design by Melanie Feddersen, i2i Design
Typeset by Melanie Feddersen, i2i Design
Manufactured/Printed in Singapore by Imago

10 9 8 7 6 5 4 3 2 1